Palgrave Studies in Economic History

Series Editor
Kent Deng, London School of Economics, London, UK

Palgrave Studies in Economic History is designed to illuminate and enrich our understanding of economies and economic phenomena of the past. The series covers a vast range of topics including financial history, labour history, development economics, commercialisation, urbanisation, industrialisation, modernisation, globalisation, and changes in world economic orders.

Elisabetta Merlo · Ivan Paris

The Italian Fashion System

The Role of Institutions and Institutional Change, 1940s–1980s

palgrave
macmillan

Elisabetta Merlo
Department of Social and Political Sciences
Bocconi University
Milan, Italy

Ivan Paris
Department of Economics and Management
University of Brescia
Brescia, Italy

ISSN 2662-6497 ISSN 2662-6500 (electronic)
Palgrave Studies in Economic History
ISBN 978-3-031-52374-8 ISBN 978-3-031-52375-5 (eBook)
https://doi.org/10.1007/978-3-031-52375-5

This Palgrave Macmillan imprint is published by the registered company Springer Nature Switzerland AG
The registered company address is: Gewerbestrasse 11, 6330 Cham, Switzerland

Paper in this product is recyclable.

Introduction

Fashion has long been a subject of inquiry in the fields of economic history and business history. Since the 1980s, and with increasing frequency in the past two decades, numerous studies have been published that address this topic in many countries and from various perspectives, paying equal attention to both the pre-industrial era and the contemporary age. Economic and business historians are now fully aware of the role played by fashion as a driver of economic change and of the key actors involved. This awareness extends to other disciplinary areas, and that of fashion is now a research field with a high degree of autonomy.

In Italy, the turning point was marked by the publication in 2003 of the collective volume titled *La moda*, edited by economic historians Marco Belfanti and Fabio Giusberti.[1] This extensive work marked the definitive awareness of the relevance of the subject and the beginning of an intense period of research on the economic function of fashion, with particular focus on the reasons behind the success of so-called *Made in Italy*. The theme has been approached from multiple angles: from the genesis of Italian specialization in the sector to the specifics of production organization; from national and international commercial strategies to various forms of representation of interests, up to interactions with demand and consumer culture. The goal is to delve ever deeper into one

[1] Belfanti and Giusberti (2003).

of the most dynamic sectors of post-war Italian economy, which today still enjoys considerable success in foreign markets.

Another potential research topic concerns the various institutional actors that have fostered the growth and the success of the Italian fashion. This is a topic that has been only marginally addressed and suffers from the absence of a comprehensive work that, even in a comparative context, highlights what is considered a unique feature of the Italian fashion system. With this book, we aim to inform the international scientific community of the distinctly polycentric nature of Italian fashion through a more detailed analysis of the roles played by the numerous institutions involved. The role of institutions in economic growth is acknowledged by both economists and economic historians alike. It is a topic that has been discussed for some time but was revitalized by the work of Douglass C. North, published in 1990.[2] Some of the studies that followed have gone so far as to link the wealth or poverty of entire nations to the quality of their institutional framework.[3] If such an approach is valid for entire economic systems, it is all the more applicable to individual sectors of production.

While fully aware of how the very definition of institutions, whether economic or otherwise, lends itself to multiple interpretations, tied to various theoretical approaches and different schools of thought, 'organizations' can be included within the realm of institutions. Here, organizations are understood to be groups of people who come together to achieve one or more common objectives that are difficult to attain individually.[4] The so-called business interest associations (BIAs), being organizations comprised of entrepreneurs in their business roles, are part of this category.[5] In the Italian fashion industry, as the reader will also see in this book, there were BIAs dedicated to the protection of specific entrepreneurial interests. However, among the most active participants in the broader process of enhancement of fashion were a multitude of entities and associations of different nature, with distinct characteristics and objectives—and in some cases, broader—than those of a trade organization. This situation was a symptom of the extreme dynamism and

[2] North (1990).

[3] Acemoglu and Robinson (2012).

[4] Hodgson (2006, 8–13).

[5] Lanzalaco (2007).

economic significance of the Italian fashion industry, which attracted the interests of many (public authorities included).[6] However, the involvement of a multiplicity of BIAs, bodies, and various associations was also the result of a situation that was still fragmented in terms of production and commercial structure. In some cases, in particular, certain activities and their associated interests were concentrated in specific regions of the country.

Both economic and business historians and other social scientists have only been partially interested in these forms of economic organization between hierarchy and market. For a long time, influenced by the studies of Alfred Chandler, more attention has been given to the large enterprises rather than other intermediate governance structures.[7] This perspective has gradually been called into question, and more recent studies have highlighted their ability, under certain conditions, to extend beyond specific interests in order to promote the broader process of economic development.[8] For this reason, the attention of social scientists for them has grown, along with studies that address the topic from a historical and comparative perspective. These studies do not neglect regional or local contexts and place particular emphasis on the contribution made in terms of economic growth.[9]

Attention towards the numerous organizations and associations engaged in the protection, promotion, and development of Italian fashion is quite recent. In particular, the results of those works aiming to provide an overview of the phenomenon remain relatively modest.[10] This depends on the short time frame considered, which inevitably limits its explanatory potential. Moreover, it is primarily due to the approach that, while meritoriously attempting a comparison between the Italian and French cases, heavily draws on previous works regarding the former,[11] yet fails to offer an interpretation that extends beyond the simple narration of largely known facts and events. Rather than delving into the detailed activities of each of the main organizations involved, this book aims to

[6] See Pinchera (2011).

[7] Scranton and Horowitz (1997).

[8] I.e., Doner and Schneider (2000).

[9] I.e., Fraboulet-Rousselier, Locatelli, and Tedeschi (2013).

[10] Di Giangirolamo (2021).

[11] I.e., White (2000), Merlo (2003), Paris (2006), Pinchera (2009), Capalbo (2012).

highlight their different governance models and their long-term evolution in relation to the transformation of the surrounding environment. This approach allows for the observation of complex relational dynamics from a different perspective and enables an original understanding of the contribution made by Italian fashion institutions to the establishment of a stable, efficient, and internationally competitive fashion system.

In this context, institutions should be understood by seeking a thorough demonstration of their economic function, documenting how the potential growth of the Italian fashion industry is linked to a specific institutional configuration. Recent studies have confirmed that a qualitative and interpretative approach could be beneficial, provided that, grounded in rigorous empirical analysis and taking a long-term perspective, it encompasses all the activities of an institution (or an organization) and its interactions with the surrounding environment.[12] It is therefore necessary to consider not only the position of those who, willingly or not, are excluded, but also their potential inefficiency, which can lead to forms of resistance to change, the failure of the institution itself, and a potential crisis in the sector under study.

The Italian fashion system became well established in the three decades following World War II and substantially contributed to the international success of Italian fashion. While the 1950s was a period of formation, marked by the organization of the first Italian Fashion Show in Florence in 1951, the 1960s saw a transformation, with the industry increasingly dictating the pace and timing of development. The 1970s marked the definitive consecration, with Milan becoming the new capital and one of the world's most important fashion hubs.

Explanations for the rise of Italian fashion to international prominence have typically emphasized the creativity and charisma of fashion designers, the evolution of fashion demand (in Italy and outside), the impact of fashion fairs, the peculiarities of the Italian business model, and the uniqueness of its industrial background. Academic literature still lacks a comprehensive history of the Italian fashion system viewed from an institutional perspective. This book aims to enrich the existing interpretative framework by paying attention to the main institutional actors, a controversial and still underexplored aspect of the story. The focus is on institutions, but the book also examines the supply and demand side

[12] Decker, Kipping, and Wadhwani (2015).

because analysing the broader context is the first step in understanding institutional change. As a result, the reader will find many references to these topics along all the chapters of the book.

Interdisciplinary in scope, the book is structured in three chapters. The first one summarizes events crucial to the knowledge of the history of Italian fashion. In this overview, neophytes will find a concise description of Italy's emergence into the realm of fashion and the explanation of the stages of its transformation from negligible presence into top player in the international arena after World War II. Expert readers, instead, will find an unconventional approach to the history of Italian fashion, as the focus will be on the making of the Italian fashion system—defined as the result of vertical integration of sectors comparable in terms of production processes and horizontal integration of sectors that produce different kinds of goods depending on consumer preferences—rather than on Italian fashion itself.

The second chapter examines the various organizations directly involved in the management of Italian fashion. Analysing the geography of Italian fashion is the first step in assessing its fragmentation from an institutional perspective. All representatives of the main components of the fashion system have undertaken the challenging task of regulating their specific interests to reconcile them with the broader goal of strengthening the entire sector and making fashion a stable source of economic growth. The analysis sheds light on a plurality of contrasting and overlapping governance models which, in some cases, were even competing among themselves.

The third chapter examines the impact of the changes described in the previous chapters on the institutional framework of Italian fashion. The downsizing or failure of the main organizations previously involved in the protection and promotion of a strategically important sector for the country's economic development was accompanied by the emergence of new institutional actors. In particular, we shall analyse the emergence of the stylist as the main result of an extended process of institutional change. The pivot of a revitalized network of relationships, the stylist completed the formation process of the Italian fashion system, thereby expanding and consolidating the success of Italian fashion in international markets.

Elisabetta Merlo
Ivan Paris

References

Acemoglu, Daron, and James A. Robinson, 2012. *Why nations fail. The origin of power, prosperity and poverty*. New York: Crown Publishers.

Belfanti, Carlo Marco, and Fabio Giusberti, eds. 2003. *La moda*. Storia d'Italia, Annali 19. Turin: Einaudi.

Capalbo, Cinzia. 2012. *Storia della moda a Roma. Sarti, culture e stili di una capitale dal 1871 a oggi*. Rome: Donzelli.

Decker, Stephanie, Matthias Kipping, and R. Daniel Wadhwani. 2015. "New Business Histories! Plurality in Business History Research Methods." *Business History* 57 (1): 30–40.

Di Giangirolamo, Gianluigi. 2021. *Institutions for Fashion. Public and Private Intervention in Italy and France (1945–1965)*. Milan: Bruno Mondadori.

Doner, Richard F., and Ben Schneider. 2000. "Business Associations and Economic Development: Why Some Associations Contribute More Than Others." *Business and Politics* 2 (3): 261–88.

Fraboulet-Rousselier, Danièle, Andrea Maria Locatelli, and Paolo Tedeschi, eds. 2013. *Historical and International Comparison of Business Interest Associations, 19th–20th Centuries*. Brussels: Peter Lang.

Hodgson, Geoffrey M. 2006. "What Are Institutions?" *Journal of Economic Issue* XL (1): 1–25.

Lanzalaco, Luca. 2007. "Business interest associations." In *The Oxford handbook of Business History*, edited by G. Jones and J. Zeitlin, 293–315. New York: Oxford University Press.

Merlo, Elisabetta. 2003. *Moda italiana. Storia di un'industria dall'Ottocento ad oggi*. Venice: Marsilio.

North, Douglass C., 1990. *Institution, institutional change and economic performance*. Cambridge: Cambridge University Press.

Paris, Ivan. 2006. *Oggetti cuciti. L'abbigliamento pronto in Italia dal primo dopoguerra agli anni Settanta*. Milan: Franco Angeli.

Pinchera, Valeria. 2009. *La moda in Italia e in Toscana. Dalle origini alla globalizzazione*. Venice: Marsilio.

Pinchera, Valeria. 2011. "I provvedimenti per la ripresa economica nel secondo dopoguerra. Promozione e sostegno della moda italiana (1945–1970)." In *L'intervento dello Stato nell'economia italiana. Continuità e cambiamenti (1922–1956)*, edited by A. Cova and G. Fumi, 485–514. Milan: Franco Angeli.

Scranton, Philip, and Roger Horowitz. 1997. "The Future of Business History: An Introduction." *Business and Economic History* 26 (1): 1–4.

White, Nicola. 2000. *Reconstructing Italian Fashion. America and the Development of the Italian Fashion Industry*. Oxford-New York: Berg.

Contents

List of Tables

CHAPTER 1

The History of Italian Fashion

Abstract This chapter charts and summarizes events crucial to the understanding of the history of Italian fashion. The focus will be on the creation of the Italian fashion system, defined as the result of the vertical integration of sectors comparable in terms of production processes, and the horizontal integration of sectors that produce different kinds of goods depending on consumer preferences. This analysis is preliminary to the understanding of institutions as key actors in the Italian fashion system rise and development, with which the following chapters deal in-depth.

Keywords Italian fashion · Textile and clothing industry · American market

1.1 The 1950s: Italian Fashion Attracts an American Audience

The buyer Giovanni Battista Giorgini organized the first collective Italian *couturier(e)s* fashion show in 1951. Fashion historians consider the event as the birth of Italian fashion. How could an individual, private initiative taken by a single, commercial intermediary successfully challenge the well-established French and English counterparts? This section answers

E. Merlo and I. Paris, *The Italian Fashion System*, Palgrave Studies in Economic History, https://doi.org/10.1007/978-3-031-52375-5_1

the question by placing emphasis on both the exceptional historic circumstances and the institutional vacuum in which the first Italian Fashion Shows took place.

In 1951, Giovanni Battista Giorgini, a buyer who had already entered the US market in the 1920s by exporting handmade Tuscan products, organized the first collective Italian *couturier(e)s'* fashion show at his residence in Florence. He invited buyers from the most important American department stores, including I. Magnin, B. Altman, Bergdorf Goodman, and Henry Morgan. The event was held just after the French fashion dates, in order to entice American buyers to prolong their stay in Europe to include a visit to Florence, and was conceived as an opportunity to celebrate the Renaissance as the time when Italy lead the artistic world. Success exceeded the best expectations to the point that for the second show, held in July 1951, Giorgini obtained the use of Florence's Grand Hotel, where 600 dresses were unveiled. One year later, fashion shows started to be staged in the evocative *Sala Bianca* of the famous Florentine *Palazzo Pitti*, a venue that reinforced the myth of the Renaissance being the origin of Italian aesthetic culture. By accepting Giorgini's invitation, the Italian fashion houses ended (although only temporarily) the custom of presenting their shows individually, each in its own *atelier*, a few weeks after the Parisian events in order to have the time to acknowledge and develop new trends launched on the catwalks of the undisputed capital of fashion. Buyers from prominent American department stores who attended the Florentine shows welcomed Italian fashion as a rising star in the fashion world. Not surprisingly, fashion historians unanimously regard the *Sala Bianca* as the birthplace of Italian fashion, with Giorgini named as its father.[1]

The narrative of the birth of Italian fashion is neither wholly convincing nor comprehensive. Although the rise of Italian fashion since the early 1950s has been nothing short of staggering, it is unlikely that it sprung from nothing. Looking closer, Florence's ascendance to the status of international fashion capital raises questions such as: How and why did Italian fashion become so successful so fast? Why did Americans like Italian fashion? How did an individual, private initiative taken up by a single, commercial intermediary successfully challenge the well-established foreign counterparts?

[1] Vergani (1992), Pinchera (2009, 23–80), Pinchera and Rinallo (2020), Calanca and Segre Reinach (2021).

Reasonably, the leap forward that Italian fashion took following the end of World War II was based on pre-existing strengths and weaknesses. The list of strengths includes Italy's heritage of art and culture, well-established manufacturing traditions, and the industry's deep understanding of fashion both as a transnational cultural phenomenon and as a product with intrinsic artistic value.

Although the Florentine fashion shows provide a self-evident example of marketing through history,[2] it is equally true that Italy's heritage of art and culture really provided (the few) Italian *couturier(e)s* with a plentiful source of inspiration and paved the way for international recognition. Rosa Genoni, Maria Monaci Gallenga, and Germana Marucelli—the pioneers who lead the ascendance of Italian fashion to an international standing—are cases in point.[3]

Italy's heritage of art and culture was not the only asset Italian fashion could capitalize on. Rather, such heritage was enriched with well-established manufacturing traditions that embraced a wide range of activities—including printing, embroidering, and finishing—as well as artisanal skills related to the use of materials such as silver and gold threads, glass and gems to decorate clothing, and leather to produce accessories. Among the crucial links in the entire value chain, textiles had historically been a strong sector within the Italian economy and had enjoyed a good reputation internationally since the late Middle Ages, the time when Lombardy and Tuscany were leading centres of silk and wool production. Textiles played a vital role in nineteenth-century Italian industrialization. In the period following political unification (1861), Italy saw growth in the major economic indicators, such as industrial output and exports, with the textile industry at the forefront of its industrial expansion. In the 1870s, strict protectionist barriers succeeded in keeping the domestic market for medium and low-quality wool and cotton cloth for domestic manufacturers, thus paving the way for the industrial development. The annual rate of growth in the production of wool and cotton increased in the following years, ultimately allowing Italian manufacturers

[2] Belfanti (2015).

[3] On Monaci Gallenga see De Guttry et al. (2018), Masiola and Cittadini (2020); on Genoni see Fiorentini Capitani (1996), Venturelli (1997), Mingardo (2013), Boneschi (2014), Paulicelli (2017); on Marucelli see Fiorentini Capitani (1991, 10), Steele (1994, 497), Morini (2005, 271).

to begin production for foreign markets.[4] At the end of the century, this industrial growth resulted in most Italian firms being active in traditional, labour-intensive sectors, a characteristic that persists to this day.[5]

Along with cultural heritage and manufacturing traditions, the precursors of the advent of Italian fashion shared a deep understanding of fashion as a transnational cultural phenomenon and as a product endowed with autonomous artistic value and dignity. The intimate Italian involvement in the cultural movements that spread through Europe during the *Belle Époque* clearly emerged in the early twentieth century. In 1902, Turin hosted the first International Exhibition of Modern Decorative Arts which demonstrated the Italian participation in European modernism represented by the British *Arts and Crafts* and French *Art Nouveau* movements. In 1906, Milan aimed to consolidate Italian participation in European modernism with the opening of its international exhibition which welcomed "retrospective" creations. The Milanese approach reflected the prevailing cultural orientation in Italy at the time and was sensitive to the cultural avant-garde as well as to the exploitation of historical and artistic heritage.[6]

If the conducive prerequisites for the emergence of Italian fashion existed well before the mid-twentieth century, weaknesses were just as evident. The first concerned the lack of national identity as a source of inspiration of genuinely Italian fashion.[7]

The list of weaknesses also includes the clothing industry's backwardness, which persisted throughout the first half of the twentieth century, and is the key to understanding why attempts to establish a truly Italian fashion failed during this period. In the year when Italian fashion took its first steps on the catwalks of Florence, the new born Italian fashion sector was therefore still completely lacking in any industrial consistency.[8]

Weaknesses became fully apparent in the 1920s and 1930s, when Fascism strove to emancipate fashion from French influence. In order to

[4] Fenoaltea (1998, 2000, 2001, 2002).

[5] Merlo (2003b).

[6] On the exhibitions in Turin and Milan see De Spigliati (1902), Fratini (1971), Bossaglia et al. (1994), Levra and Roccia (2003), Piazzoni (1995), Redondi and Zocchi (2006), Misiano (2014).

[7] Merlo (2021).

[8] Gamberini (1957), Merlo (2003a, 670).

overcome the importance of France, Fascism evoked (ancient Roman) classical themes to resuscitate the ailing national identity, boosted civil uniforms to provide a market for the boom in the clothing industry, and promoted behaviours and practices that ensured the entire fashion value chain was under Italian control. Results were disappointing, as Italian fashion remained nothing but a facet of the bombastic Fascist rhetoric of the time.[9]

The post-war climate eventually allowed the resolution of the imbalance between strengths and weaknesses that prevented Italian fashion from emerging until the mid-twentieth century. The first Italian Fashion Shows took place while the European Recovery Program (1948–1952) was in force. The primary impact of American aid was political and cultural, rather than economic. These aid strategies were the means of spreading the gospel of productivity and growth, which underpinned the Program, throughout Western Europe, changing both methods of production and models of consumption.[10]

Americanization, i.e., the process of assimilation of American customs and values, deeply affected international trade, bringing Europe and especially Italy closer to the United States. The international geography of fashion was also influenced, as America's enthusiastic response to Giorgini's initiatives proves. While London emerged as the most innovative centre of fashion design and production, and New York repositioned itself from a manufacturing centre to an influential fashion hub, Paris still suffered from the deprivations of war.[11] The new opportunities that grew out of the influence of the American lifestyle and clothing allowed Italy to become a major beneficiary of the decline experienced by Paris during the war. The French reaction reverted to pre-war splendour. In 1947, Dior's New Look was launched. The New Look was a resounding success among the war-weary population, for whom it meant the revival of the opulence of the early twentieth century.[12] The promotion of an exaggeratedly feminine figure was in keeping with the prevalent view that women, after their participation in the war effort, had to return to the home as full-time home-makers and mothers. Furthermore, the revivalist style implied

[9] Gnoli (2000), Paulicelli (2004), Lupano and Vaccari (2009).

[10] Tiratsoo and Tomlison (1997), Kipping and Bjarna (1998), Fauri (2010).

[11] Veillon (1990).

[12] Palmer (2009), Jones and Pouillard (2013).

the use of large quantities of fabric thus stimulating the struggling textile industry.

In Italy, a strong dichotomy developed between the refined yet overly structured elegance of French tailoring and the casual, sporty comfort of American design. Italian *couturier(e)s* understood the need for clothing that incorporated the most appealing aspects of both, that is, for more accessible, comfortable, and yet equally refined and tailored collections. The textile industry played a major role in this effort by venturing into collaborations with the representatives of the emerging generation of fashion designers. The majority of Italian tailors, however, remained ambivalent. The will to keep faith with the image of high fashion designed and made to be worn by an elite clientele conflicted with the nascent awareness that their creations, purchased by American buyers, would clothe thousands of people. As a result, styles became easier, but were not modernized. By mitigating the desire to be luxurious, Italian fashion became less conspicuous, therefore more balanced and more affordable, while also more bourgeois and traditionalist than French *haute couture*, and was still imbued with artisanal credos.

The Florentine shows did not succeed in creating a modern industrial business. The garments shown were still largely (although not exclusively) the work of highly trained tailors and seamstresses performing manual activities in small-scale workshops, rather than the result of large-scale industrial production. Giorgini himself never really managed to make—and probably was not even interested in making—the shift from artisan to industrial production.[13] Those who accepted Giorgini's invitation to show their collections on the Florentine catwalks in 1951 were instead fully representative of a new kind of fashion, the so-called *moda boutique* (boutique fashion).

Boutique fashion was a distinctly Italian creative experience. It was produced in (small) batches and positioned itself between high fashion and ready-to-wear. The boutique model combined the qualities of craftsmanship and materials with the potential of mass production and the branding of a renowned tailor. The perfect blend of quality, exclusivity, and mass production, even if lacking in uniqueness, contributed to its international success. However, it still maintained an essentially artisanal dimension. For this reason, the price of boutique fashion was still high,

[13] Pinchera and Rinallo (2020).

albeit lower than that of *haute couture*.[14] Of course, there were exceptions, such as creations by prominent *couturier(e)s* like Emilio Pucci, which could be close to 200 USD (in line, however, with prices of ready-to-wear garments produced for the American market by French fashion houses such as Dior).[15]

This explains why boutique fashion found commercial success in only a few countries, where, for many consumers, it represented the sole means to access the prestigious fashion houses. The United States was one of these countries, primarily because the clean lines of boutique fashion adapted well to the creation of models intended for (large-scale) industrial production. Simultaneously, this intermediate production appealed greatly to emancipated American women because it was not only easy to wear but also characterized by the quality of traditional Italian craftsmanship and the allure of well-known *couturier(e)s*. Simplicity and glamour were the keys to winning over the dynamic young American woman, whose appreciation of boutique fashion was evident through the keen interest of buyers starting from the very first editions of the Italian Fashion Show in Florence. Boutique fashion went beyond offering simple garments, moving towards a total look that also included accessories. For example, Emilio Pucci granted licenses for products such as shoes and perfumes.

Americanization also affected the organization of textile and clothing production. American aid allowed the textile industry to start a process of intensive technological modernization and to integrate itself vertically into the manufacture of ready-made garments by adopting methods suitable for mass production. Throughout the late 1940s and 1950s, American companies welcomed visits from European colleagues and potential competitors who wished to study their advanced systems. In 1956, the US Department of Labor compiled a report specifically intended for European production managers on the manufacture of women's dresses.

In the mid-1950s, a handful of Italian clothing firms—including Max Mara, Lubiam, Marzotto, and GFT—started mass production, a move that made industry responsible for a profound change in fashion consumption. The majority were textile companies which took advantage of the aid received from the Marshall Plan in order to initiate an intense

[14] White (2000, 44, 49–50), Paris (2006a, 218–31).

[15] Pouillard (2021, 826).

process of technological modernization. For them, the production of ready-made garments represented not only a channel which could absorb the increase in textile production, but also a sounding board for research, design, and experimentation with innovations in distribution, marketing, and manufacturing. Specifically, standardization coincided with the adoption of sizes. The system of sizes adopted in Italy echoed American commercial standards by stressing standardization as a means to supply a common basis for fair competition focused on factors such as quality, style, and fit. Following its American predecessor, the Italian system of sizes aimed to lay the technical foundations for a new concept of ready-made garment based on clothing sizes rather than on body measurements. The garment would no longer aim to imitate made-to-measure and would ultimately be more sensitive to fashion changes rather than to tailoring accuracy.[16]

Innovations in production, retail, and advertising greatly affected the culture and economy of clothing. The common belief that a ready-made garment was similar to a reused, second-hand piece of clothing had hindered acceptance for a long time. New retail formats and innovative advertising strategies played a crucial role in changing this mindset, allowing ready-made clothing to be recognized as reputable. In an effort to make ready-made clothing fashionable as well, industrial firms approached *couturier(e)s* with the aim of making mass-produced clothing commercially appealing to fashion-sensitive female customers. Although still tentative and mostly unsuccessful, this approach paved the way for the ensuing closer relationship between creativity and industry.[17]

The 1950s coincided with a period that saw the establishment of relationships between textile producers and manufacturers of man-made fibres. By using fabrics produced domestically, Italian fashion houses gained increasing autonomy from the French leadership in fashion. During this phase, which could be defined as the industrial qualification of high fashion, at the most important fashion shows, the great Italian designers of the time linked their names to those of some of the most famous textile producers (wool, cotton, silk, and artificial fibres). At the IX Fashion Show at the *Sala Bianca*, Emilio Pucci presented his designs made with Marzotto fabrics, Capucci with those of Il Fabbricone Lanificio

[16] Merlo (2015).

[17] Merlo (2014).

Italiano, Carosa with those of Filande e Tessiture Costa and Rhodiatoce, Veneziani with those of Bemberg and Lanificio Fratelli Faudella, and Antonelli with those of Textiloses & Textiles (a French company with a commercial branch in Milan and factories in Lombardy) and Rhodiatoce. High fashion ventured into the experimental world of collaboration between fashion and industry with relationships based on the exclusive supply of products. These relationships were sometimes one-offs while others evolved into long-term alliances, such as that between Cesare Guidi and Lanificio Faliero Sarti which made the designer famous for the originality of the fabrics used to make his suits. In other cases, the collaboration between industry and fashion was a partnership which aimed to discover new materials. One of the pioneers of this type of collaboration was Emilio Pucci who, together with Legler, created artificial and synthetic velvets for sports trousers, and with Cotonificio Valle Susa produced the patterned "wally pliss" material. With Mabu and E. Boselli, Pucci created a jersey made from silk organza, ideal for making ladies garments which were crease-free and space-saving. Generally, these collaborative relationships between fashion and industry changed the course of history for the businesses involved. As a matter of fact, Americans did not associate Italian fashion only with affordability, taste, and careful tailoring. They were also greatly impressed by the creative use of man-made fibres, either alone or in combination with natural materials.[18]

Although the Florentine shows did not succeed in creating a modern industrial business, they certainly aimed to create a showcase for the novelty of Italian fashion, sources of inspiration, creative partnerships, and its foundation in local traditions. As opposed to France, where fashion was firmly linked to Paris, various Italian towns, each of which boasted different capabilities, aspired to be crowned *the* capital of Italian fashion. Every town had its own specialization deeply rooted in its history. Rome, for example, was synonymous with Italian high fashion; Florence's variety of handicrafts was deemed the epitome of elegance; while Turin was considered the cradle of industry, and Milan the city where industry and design merged. Associations comprising *couturier(e)s*, entrepreneurs, and representatives of economic organizations proliferated, reflecting the plurality of the alleged capitals of Italian fashion, each competing to be the lone standard-bearer for the industry.

[18] Savi (2023, 29–33).

This competition among the Italian fashion capitals fed parochial rivalries which resulted in the withdrawal from the Florentine catwalks of some well-known high fashion and boutique fashion designers. However, the number of buyers and press attending the *Pitti* fashion shows increased considerably, reaching a total of 600 people from 13 countries in 1959. These figures provide further clues to the reasons why the Florentine shows—an individual, private initiative seized by a single, commercial intermediary—were such a resounding success. They provide evidence of Giorgini's tireless networking activity and reflect the exceptional commercial background he relied upon. In 1956, the *Associazione Nazionale Italiana Buying Offices* (ANIBO, National Buying Offices Association) was established in Florence. Giorgini was its first President. At the end of the 1960s, almost two hundred buying offices operated in Florence. They created a tight network of relationships and contacts between the North American distribution system and the industry, which was made up mainly of artisan enterprises scattered around Florence and within the Tuscan region. These "anonymous tastemakers" played a crucial role in introducing American customers to Italian fashion.[19]

By the end of the 1950s, Europe had finally emerged from the shortages and deprivations of the immediate post-war years. Italy was no exception. The national market grew with the increase in private demand. A huge rise in income fuelled an unprecedented boom in consumption, with money being spent on a larger variety of goods and services, including those aimed at improving the population's health and quality of life (e.g., houses, furniture, and domestic appliances), as well as those that the Italian population deemed symbols of the modern way of living, such as ready-to-wear clothing, specifically menswear. The growing prosperity of Western countries was to result in the emergence of the consumer society of the 1960s.

1.2 The 1960s: A Crucial Decade

At first glance, the 1960s may seem merely like a transitionary period between the pyrotechnic beginnings of the Florentine shows and the revolutionary fashion of the 1970s. This section deals with the main economic, social, cultural, and institutional facts that made the 1960s a

[19] Stanfill (2018), Pinchera (2009), Marcucci (2004).

crucial decade for the ensuing development of the Italian fashion industry, paving the way for a new phase of the history of the Italian fashion system to begin.

To deal with the 1960s in detail requires a comprehensive examination of the genuine economic, social, cultural, and institutional factors that influenced the development of the Italian fashion industry, rather than relying solely on general considerations of the well-known peculiarities of a decade marked by significant transformations.

In this pivotal decade, the foundations of the Italian fashion system were laid. Many factors favoured and supported this process. Technology, for instance, had a significant impact on production processes and materials. New artificial and synthetic fibres, with their unique characteristics, opened up new possibilities for creating practical, comfortable, and affordably priced clothing.[20] Recent analyses of the dynamics of Europe's long economic boom after World War II have generally acknowledged the leading role played by the transfer of US technology and organizational practice within a broad process of catch-up and convergence.[21] The contribution of the United States to the modernization of the Italian textile and clothing industry continued to be substantial. On the one hand, there was a constant flow of technical and managerial knowledge, benefiting both the textile and ready-to-wear industries. On the other hand, as mentioned in the previous section, the United States provided access to its vast and prosperous market for Italian products, starting with exclusive and high-quality productions such as high fashion and boutique fashion. These and other factors pushed towards increasingly large-scale production (the so-called ready-made fashion), characterized by sound material and immaterial qualities. The parallel growth of the domestic market and European demand further reinforced this trend. In Italy, the increase in per capita income facilitated the growth of the ready-to-wear sector.[22] According to the *Associazione Italiana Industriali dell'Abbigliamento* (AIIA, Italian Clothing Industry Association), by the mid-1960s the market share of ready-made fashion had surpassed fifty

[20] Blaszczyk (2007), Handley (1999), Savi (2023, 29–33). On the Italian case see Colli (2003).

[21] For a wider review of this literature see Zeitlin (2000). On the impact of the American model of production and consumption in Europe see also De Grazia (2005), Schröter (2005).

[22] Felice and Vecchi (2015).

percent. Compared to the previous decade, the turnover had quadrupled, and the value of exports had grown more than eight times (in contrast, spending on tailor-made garments had fallen by more than 25%).[23]

For the purposes of this book, the demand for clothing deserves particular attention.[24] The rapid and profound changes in demand deeply impacted the supply structure, altering the existing power dynamics. This transformation fully manifested itself in the second half of the 1960s, by which time all the previously mentioned factors had already shown their effects. Unlike previous periods, the new structure that emerged no longer revolved around the exclusivity of high fashion (until then the focal point of the creative phase and a manifesto for the entire production chain). Instead, it was based on the 'democratization' ensured by industrial clothing production for the mass market. The ready-to-wear sector, which adapted to meet the demands of new consumers, gradually replaced high fashion, even in terms of leadership in taste, demonstrating unexpected skill in managing the 'fashion variable.' In this new scenario, all the organizations involved in the governance of Italian fashion, faced with increasing pressure, did not always fully comprehend the ongoing changes. Responding to the new stimuli in an inconsistent manner, these entities were condemned to marginalization and, in some cases, failure. This analysis thus starts with the premise of the centrality of demand to examine the meaning of 'system' in the Italian fashion industry and to interpret not only its formation but also its institutional aspect. Maintaining focus on the demand side, this section describes the context from which the new Italian fashion system emerged and became established.

According to Kawamura, "fashion is a system of institutions, organizations, groups, producers, events, and practices, all of which contribute to the making of fashion, which is different from dress or clothing".[25] The first step is, therefore, to provide a satisfactory definition of 'system', applied within a diverse sector that includes a variety of goods and involves multiple actors. The concept of 'system' is broader and more flexible than that of 'sector'. It identifies a range of products which are coordinated based on both the technical and organizational characteristics of the production process (i.e., the available technology) and the consumer's

[23] AIIA (1985, 9–10, 12–3, 15).

[24] Paris (2010a).

[25] Kawamura (2005, 48).

preferences (i.e., the socio-economic dimension of fashion).[26] Tracing its boundaries, therefore, depends on assessments from both demand and supply sides. The system thus emerges as the result of vertical integration of sectors with similar process phases and horizontal integration of supply chains for different products. While vertical integration is ensured (in part) by process similarity, the pivotal question revolves around what ensures horizontal integration. A significant part of the process in forming the Italian fashion system revolved around establishing a network of stable relationships, both vertical and horizontal. Understanding which factor provided the stability of the new system is, therefore, crucial.

The second step involves analysing the state of relationships between various actors in the Italian fashion industry. Some attempts at vertical integration had been made in the previous decade, but it was only during the 1960s that the need for horizontal expansion of the supply chain became more pressing.

As seen in the previous section, the textile industry was the first to attempt vertical expansion.[27] The objective was to capitalize on the increased productivity generated by technological and organizational innovations in the spinning and weaving stages. Expanding the supply chain downstream to include ready-to-wear production was, therefore, a consequence of the changes that occurred in the structure of supply.

An illustrative example is the case of Manifattura Lane Gaetano Marzotto, a family business that had already initiated industrial production of both men's and women's clothing in newly equipped facilities as early as the 1950s.[28] The case of Marzotto is significant because the process of vertical integration extended all the way to the distribution phase, involving the direct management of their own retail outlets or through agreements with other commercial enterprises. The investments required for this operation were substantial, even considering the financial resources made available through post-war reconstruction plans. For a facility of minimal size, capable of producing around one hundred garments per day, the estimated cost was approximately 200 million ITL (Italian Lira).[29] The frequent trips made to the United States by certain

[26] Ciabattoni (1976, 23–30).

[27] Merlo (2003b, 83–91).

[28] Roverato (1986), Bairati (1986), Brunetti and Camuffo (1994).

[29] Settimi (1964, 25).

members of the family that owned the business confirm a genuine willingness to invest in a sector which was deemed profitable, rather than merely to exploit technological and financial contingencies.[30] The objective of these journeys was to acquire the necessary know-how to replicate in Italy what had already been accomplished to an excellent standard in the United States, in terms of both production organization and product quality. The clothing produced by Marzotto under the *Fuso d'Oro* brand ushered in a new era for Italian fashion, marking the beginning of a transition process that would transform the industrial craftsmanship of the traditional local dressmaker of the first half of the twentieth century into a genuine industry.[31]

The case of Marzotto was not the only experiment in vertical integration initiated by textile industries. The Gruppo Tessile Miroglio (GTM) also developed a ready-to-wear line in 1955 (with the *Vestebene* brand), while Lanificio Rossi entered this market in the early 1960s, participating in the management of the famous *Lebole* brand.[32] The case of GTM is worth mentioning due to its use of in-house produced artificial fibres (such as rayon). The objective was to exploit the multiple advantages these fibres offer to create affordable, lightweight, and durable garments that were also comfortable and appealing to wear.[33] The fabric design was pleasing, reflecting the well-known quality of Italian textile production. The experience of GTM foreshadowed the fruitful connection that would be established in the 1960s between the ready-to-wear industry and artificial and synthetic fibres, which had already been successfully produced in Italy in the interwar period by companies such as Snia Viscosa, one of the sector's leading international players.[34] This partnership expanded the market and encouraged the spread of new clothing items while also supporting the revival of certain traditional products. This was the case, for instance, for polyester fibres, which, due to their physical characteristics and low production costs, facilitated the industrial production of

[30] White (2000, 22).

[31] Paris (2006b).

[32] Repek (2003).

[33] Rasi (1959).

[34] Cerretano (2022).

an iconic garment like the raincoat—which achieved its greatest public success during the 1960s.[35]

Another noteworthy example of vertical integration is the pioneering collaboration between the chain of department stores La Rinascente (Italy's leading department store) and Apem (Abbigliamento Produzione Esportazione Milano), representing the union of the retail industry with the ready-to-wear sector.[36] Apem, in which La Rinascente held the majority stake, could be regarded as a large-scale enterprise. By the early 1960s, it employed approximately 800 workers and had the capacity to produce thousands of garments per day.[37] The United States played a significant role in the growth of Apem, both through a continuous flow of technology and expertise and by encouraging the production of garments tailored to the preferences of the American public.[38] Apem's production included not only large-scale output with very economical items (just over 1.5 USD wholesale) but also smaller productions with undoubtedly higher prices (up to 300 USD) while offering superior quality, therefore more suitable for the American consumer.[39]

The attempt at backward vertical integration pursued by La Rinascente and Apem represented one of the most significant innovations in the Italian fashion industry between the 1950s and 1960s. Firstly, because it is regarded as the primary (if not the only) initiative aimed at establishing a direct relationship between large-scale retail and industrial clothing production. Secondly, because it showcased the desire to *democratize* the fashion sector, which was still dominated by the exclusivity of *haute couture*.[40] Apem and La Rinascente aimed to achieve this goal by expanding the target market and enhancing the overall quality of the product, which was hindering the success of Italian ready-to-wear, especially among the female audience. This entailed investing in technology and optimizing the production process to reduce costs while

[35] Confederazione Generale dell'Industria Italiana (1958, 131–5), Comitato Italiano per il Cotone (1960), AIIA (1980).

[36] Amatori (1989), Papadia (2005).

[37] White (2000, 57–8, 64), L'Abbigliamento Italiano (AI) (1960).

[38] Rossetti (1961), Capalbi (1961). On the evolution of American fashion see Cunningham and Welters (2005).

[39] White (2000, 57).

[40] Zanetti (1960).

improving the material quality of the product. However, intervention was also necessary in the creative phase to enhance the intangible content of mass-produced clothing. The United States and the New York garment district continued to serve as the point of reference in this process.[41] It was to these manufacturers that all the major American department stores turned, commissioning clothing inspired by models purchased or exclusively designed by prestigious fashion designers (many of whom were Italian and French).

Therefore, in the early 1960s, Apem and La Rinascente were moving in the direction set by the United States, albeit on two different but converging levels. La Rinascente had already begun in the 1950s by entering into licensing agreements with some American manufacturers (Donnybrook Fashion and Henry Rosenfeld) for the production, under their direct supervision, of affordable yet high-quality ready-to-wear clothing which followed the latest fashion trends. While in the early 1960s, Apem aimed to establish collaboration agreements with renowned names in Italian high fashion (such as Galitzine, Capucci, Fabiani, and Simonetta Visconti) to simplify their designs and make them more easily reproducible on a mass scale. However, this project did not succeed. At the end of the decade, when the difficulties of the large-scale garment industry reached their peak, and industrial clothing seemed inevitably destined for the lower end of the market, Apem also faced a profound crisis and was swallowed up in the renewal process of the ready-to-wear industry.

In Italy, the relationship between large-scale retail and the clothing industry did not achieve the same results as were seen in the United States or more advanced European countries. The evident underdevelopment of the Italian retail trade in the 1950s, which had its roots in the years between the two world wars, continued to persist in the following decade.[42] The case of La Rinascente was unique in the Italian context, where products sold through large-scale retail were generally considered a compromise compared to tailor-made garments, due to a perceived lack of quality. In the first half of the decade, less than one product out of ten was sold through this commercial distribution channel. Few consumers believed they could find quality clothing in the most

[41] Soyer (2005).

[42] Zamagni (1981), Morris (1998, 1999).

popular department stores. Large-scale Italian retail was unable to cater for broader market segments because it lacked an offering structured on multiple levels of ready-made garments. Unlike countries like France, Italy lacked production of ready-to-wear garments intended for an intermediate consumer segment. Moreover, compared to the United States, there were no stores aimed specifically at more discerning consumers where they could find clothing made following the models of major *couturier(e)s*. The underdevelopment of the Italian commercial distribution network prompted large companies such as the aforementioned Marzotto to integrate downstream, establishing their own distribution network.

In the United States, buying offices of department stores played an important role in fostering relationships between high fashion, ready-to-wear, and large-scale retail. The most significant offices had branches throughout Europe (starting from Paris), and the numerous reports from major American specialist magazines (such as *Harper's Bazaar* and *Women's Wear Daily*) confirmed the involvement of buying agents from major stores in the most important fashion shows, including that organized in Florence by Giorgini. The buyers focused particularly on those models that were most suitable for mass production, and they were willing to spend considerable sums on such designs. Many Italian *couturier(e)s* were able to meet these demands and offered more competitive prices than their French competitors. However, while the American fashion press extensively covered these events, the same cannot be said for the main Italian publications, which were often more attracted to a hagiographic and parochial representation of emerging Italian fashion rather than to its commercial aspects. The Italian fashion press (and even more so the general daily and periodical press) appeared to be more interested in the world of high fashion than in the industry, which was left almost exclusively to trade publications (such as *Textilia* and *L'Abbigliamento Italiano*, the official organ of *Ente Italiano della Moda*—Italian Fashion Body).[43] This approach reflected the dualistic structure of the sector (divided between high fashion and ready-to-wear) and the resulting institutional relationships. At the very least, the more qualified press should

[43] Carrarini (2003).

have demonstrated a greater awareness of the complexity of the situation and the related issues.[44]

On the other hand, the American fashion press covered the relationships between New York manufacturers and Italian high fashion and boutique fashion designers. These contacts had been initiated very early on (Simonetta Visconti had already sold her entire spring collection to Bergdorf Goodman as early as 1951) and over time had involved many prestigious names. One of the first successful brands was *Veneziani Sport*, founded in 1951 by Jole Veneziani, who designed her models with their future mass production in mind.[45] Italian fashion houses had been following French pioneers such as Dior who, at the end of the 1940s, was designing ready-to-wear collections exclusively for the American market, reproduced in New York workshops and in American sizes.[46] Emilio Pucci deserves special mention because he began working directly with boutique fashion and can be considered the first Italian designer of high-quality ready-made garments. Winning the Neiman Marcus Award (the Oscar of fashion) in 1954, Pucci was one of the most renowned and appreciated Italian *couturier(e)s* on the other side of the Atlantic. Above all, he is credited with the success of so-called boutique fashion (or sportswear). Under his brand (Emilio), Pucci collaborated directly with prominent stores such as Neiman Marcus, Lord and Taylor, and Bonwit Teller, as well as with ready-to-wear manufacturers (Darlene in New York, for example).[47]

In this context, collaborations between the textile industry, ready-to-wear, and high fashion were the element that ensured a certain stability for the evolving fashion system. Agreements with Italian *couturier(e)s* took various forms, ranging from those involving the exclusive sale of entire collections to a single store, to those allowing for the copying or reinterpretation of a single model to adapt it to the production and taste requirements of the American market. These arrangements could also include the purchase of fabrics manufactured by Italian factories that were already working with designers, thereby promoting the national textile industry. Such conditions highlighted the gradual consolidation

[44] Archivio Storico della Camera Nazionale della Moda Italiana (ASCNMI), b. 3, *Relazione del Consiglio Direttivo all'Assemblea Generale dei soci del 16 Dicembre (1966*, 37–8).

[45] Robiola (1951), Erti (1952).

[46] Pouillard (2021, 825–30).

[47] White (2000, 50–1).

of partnerships between high fashion, boutique fashion, and the textile industry, which would remain a subject of discussion and plans for a long time. The second objective was the commercial return generated by the renowned designer's name, which, in turn, could benefit from substantial industry funding and the exclusive use of high-quality fabrics (also sought after by French fashion houses).[48] Unlike the collaborations mentioned earlier, the relationship between the textile industry and high fashion was not only occasional. Thanks in part to the establishment of the *Camera Nazionale della Moda Italiana* (National Chamber of Italian Fashion), sector agreements were entered into for the first time during the 1960s. These agreements, which will be further explored in the third chapter, provided greater stability to certain elements of the system, adding another support to the formation of the Italian fashion system. However, the road ahead was still long and ran parallel to the process of qualitative evolution of ready-made garments.

Since the 1950s, the connection with the United States allowed Italian fashion to lay the groundwork (both technically and organizationally) for the transition from an artisanal to an industrial reality. At the same time, the American market pushed for an improvement in the quality of industrial products (ready-to-wear). However, the general attitude of Italian companies did not fully comply with this requirement. The issue of industrial production quality still remained somewhat in the background. Instead, during the 1960s, it would become crucial to win over even the Italian (and European) consumer. While some prominent figures in Italian high fashion already collaborated with American manufacturers, few relationships with domestic manufacturers existed. Yet, also in this case, the potential advantages were immense. On the one hand, high fashion houses would secure significant funding, essential to safeguard the peculiarities of the creative phase and ensure production continuity. On the other hand, ready-to-wear companies could use the image of renowned *couturier(e)s* for promotional purposes and exploit their expertise to increase the overall quality of production. Understanding the reasons for an approach that differed somewhat for the Italian market compared to the American market is, therefore, a significant step.

To achieve this objective, it is necessary to analyse the structure of domestic demand, which, despite the examples of horizontal and vertical

[48] ASCNMI, b. 3, Relazione del Consiglio Direttivo all'Assemblea Generale dei soci del 29 Ottobre (1964, 67–8).

integration described in these pages, did not offer particular incentives for collaboration and the development of a stable and coherent system of relationships. In the mid-1960s, the Italian fashion sector was divided into two separate and poorly communicating parts.[49] On the one side, there was high fashion (the first level of fashion). This involved the artisanal production of tailor-made garments, catering for an elite clientele due to its exclusivity and high prices. High fashion managed the entire conceptual and stylistic evolution of fashion, refreshing lines and trends seasonally, and would later be imitated by the ready-to-wear industry (the third level of fashion). The latter had benefited from a robust yet somewhat chaotic period of growth. However, it offered a product which was highly standardized and not always of adequate quality, manufactured within large industrial facilities.[50] Between the exclusivity of high fashion and the anonymity of mass production, the aforementioned boutique fashion could be found, catering for a woman seeking a high-quality product while not desiring (or unable to afford) a wardrobe based on high fashion collections. The boutique dress, however, remained a high-end product. It was more the result of high fashion principles rather than those of industry, then different from French *prêt-à-porter*.[51]

Therefore, ready-to-wear, high fashion, and boutique fashion catered for different consumers with varying needs and budgets. This rigid segmentation of demand was reflected on the supply side and resulted in a marked polarization of the main production centres, commercial events, and promotional activities. If Florence, a reference point for boutique fashion, competed with Rome for high fashion, Milan and Turin were leaders in textiles and ready-to-wear, hosting the most important specialized trade fairs (MITAM in Milan and SAMIA in Turin).[52] Such a

[49] A more general view of Italian fashion during the twentieth century can be found in Steele (2003), Gnoli (2005), and Stanfill (2014).

[50] Paris (2006a, 307–19).

[51] The term *prêt-à-porter* refers to all the products which resulted from the requalification of ready-made clothing which started in France in the 1940s. This process was initially supported by some companies and was continued by *couturier(e)s* who consolidated its international success. On French *prêt-à-porter* see Grumbach (1993, 125–76), Lipovetsky (1987, 131–45, 151–3).

[52] Paris (2006a, 272–301), Merlo and Polese (2006), Capalbo (2012), Pinchera and Rinallo (2020), Merlo and Perugini (2020b).

structure ensured that each level of the Italian fashion industry had sufficient earnings and room for development, also beyond national borders.[53] In this context, therefore, the incentives for collaboration were few (or non-existent). However, this does not mean that there was no awareness of the importance of developing stable and long-lasting relationships, at both an individual and institutional level. This had been emphasized (in words) by the more attentive sections of the fashion press as early as the 1950s, as well as (in practice) by important *couturier(e)s* such as Jole Veneziani and Emilio Pucci, who were among the first to invest in boutique fashion and establish relationships with large-scale clothing production.[54] The same concept was still expressed in the mid-1960s by Mila Schön, one of the protagonists of the Milanese turning point in the following decade. Schön had an excellent relationship with the United States (she won the Neiman Marcus Award in 1966) and firmly believed that both high fashion and the ready-to-wear industry would have a future simply by finding common ground. The same hope had also been expressed by Giulio Goehring on behalf of the AIIA, the business association representing the interests of ready-to-wear manufacturers. At the beginning of the decade, only one-third of the total clothing consumption was provided by the industry, and the average Italian wardrobe was largely composed of handmade garments.[55] The habit of making clothes at home or sourcing them from local dressmakers could only be disrupted by offering higher-quality ready-to-wear garments, diversifying production with clothes that could fit between the exclusivity of high fashion and the anonymity that still characterized Italian ready-to-wear. The President of the AIIA (Giulio Goehring) emphasized the delay that many manufacturers showed in recognizing the signs of a potential crisis in the industry, particularly their failure to understand the changing demands of the public. Women, in particular, were beginning to prioritize fashion inspiration over traditional factors such as price, quality, and size.[56]

The suggestions made by Goehring and Schön were not embraced by the major ready-to-wear manufacturers, who attempted to ward off the crisis by boosting sales while failing to renew production. This resulted

[53] Paris (2010b).

[54] Erti (1952).

[55] Stanfill (2015).

[56] Pagani and Pavoni (1987, 32).

in the saturation of even the lower-end market segment. Only a few manufacturers managed to foresee the times ahead, starting initiatives that would soon become not just an option but a necessity for the survival of both ready-to-wear industry and high fashion.

Explaining how the creative phase was successfully integrated into the industrial production process is therefore a crucial step in understanding the evolution of the Italian fashion system. Among the early attempts at horizontal expansion of production through collaboration between fashion and industry is the partnership between Elvira Leonardi Bouyeure (known as Biki) and the Gruppo Finanziario Tessile (GFT).[57] The partnership between Biki and GFT is one of the most significant and long-lasting. It began in the late 1950s, was formalized in the early years of the following decade, and concluded in 1972. This makes it doubly interesting as it spanned the entire 1960s, reflecting the peculiarities of this period.

The goal of the collaboration was to reinvent Italian women's ready-to-wear and shift GFT's historical offering to higher-quality industrial production, including the fashion content. Initially, Biki was committed to designing the models (sketches), but in subsequent agreements, intangible assets were also included. Originally, the collaboration aimed to make the industrial product commercially appealing, taking advantage of the creativity and fame of the *couturier(e)*. Over time, the partnership evolved into true licensing agreements, which meticulously regulated their respective obligations concerning the trademark (GFT had exclusive rights to use the name Biki).

The collaboration with Biki was part of a broader project that GFT had started when the Rivetti family took ownership of the company in the early 1950s. The attention paid to the intangible content of their product followed a series of initiatives which first aimed at improving its material characteristics.[58] The objective was to make ready-to-wear competitive compared to the historical and established Italian artisanal production, not only in terms of price. The revival of the iconic men's clothing brand *Facis* was the first major step in this direction, later followed by products aimed for the women's market.

[57] Blignaut (1995), Merlo (2015).

[58] AI (1961b).

GFT was among the first to focus on the development of a new sizing system. The goal was to standardize production in order to contain costs while at the same time improving the fit of the garment.[59] Attention was directed towards the Italian consumer. The new sizing system was, in fact, the outcome of anthropometric studies carried out by GFT at its own retail outlets.[60] To support this strategy, GFT also invested in aggressive advertising campaigns and renewed its distribution network, multiplying the number of retail outlets across the country. The *Marus* stores were significantly different from traditional clothing stores, where only a partial selection of items was displayed in the windows, and inside, most products remained in boxes, forcing customers to always seek assistance from the salesperson to view the product.[61] In those stores, the entire collection was prominently displayed in spacious areas, fully accessible to customers and organized by type and size.[62] *Marus* stores thus aimed to bridge the gap between the rapid industrial growth and the modernization of retail sales that Italy needed.

Standardization had required a profound reorganization of the production process, based on the optimization of methods and work schedules. The approach dictated by GFT pushed for an increase in production scale, as evidenced by the opening of a new facility in 1963, employing over two thousand workers in the production of approximately four thousand garments per day.[63] The new system, known as "calibrated" system, included a number of sizes that were difficult to replicate in smaller-scale workshops, which instead adopted a "semi-calibrated" system. While the calibrated system could accommodate over 98% of the Italian female population, the semi-calibrated system covered less than 75%.[64] Standardization and the consequent pursuit of economies of scale, however, had to contend with increased rigidity of production, which would shift from being a strength to represent a potential weakness within a few years.

While revitalizing men's clothing and offering a viable alternative to bespoke tailoring simply required investment in the material aspects

[59] Merlo (2015).

[60] Merlo (2003a, 684–5).

[61] Morris (2003).

[62] AI (1961a), Heynold Von Graefe (1962).

[63] Rossetti (1963).

[64] Settimi (1970, 1971a, 1971b).

of the product (price, material quality, and fit), entering the women's market demanded additional effort. With the end of World War II and over two decades of fascist rule, cultures and fashion trends from European countries and from the United States flooded Italian society. The rise in income and the gradual urbanization which accompanied Italy's transformation into an industrial power accelerated changes in consumption patterns. Private consumption contributed more to growth than public consumption, with clothing and footwear being among the most significant area.[65]

In this new scenario, a growing number of discerning consumers, who were attentive and possessed greater purchasing power, began to select goods offered by the market while assessing their value in terms of status. Apparel was acquiring a higher social value, and a simple quality-price relationship was no longer sufficient to ensure commercial success.[66] In this context, fashion could only increase its role, exerting influence not only on purely aesthetic matters.[67] Some fashion experts have defined this change as the "democratization of luxury", a term that, in its apparent contradiction, highlights this significant moment of transformation.[68] The objective was no longer to add a greater number of garments to one's wardrobe, as many Italian consumers had already achieved this by the mid-1960s.[69] Luxury in clothing meant the opportunity to access garments that had significant 'fashion content', that is, a greater intangible value that was also easily identifiable and distinguishable.

The demand from the female audience was rapidly evolving, and ready-to-wear needed to be improved from an intangible perspective as well. Biki emerged as the ideal partner for GFT as she was already renowned for the simplicity of her sketches, which were more suitable than others to the needs of industrial production.[70] However, this process of re-designing the garment did not achieve the expected commercial results, featuring just the combination of Biki's name with the women's clothing brand

[65] Capuzzo (2003), Scarpellini (2011).

[66] AI (1965).

[67] Bottero (1979), English (2007), Belfanti (2008).

[68] Bottero (1969). The bibliography on the topic of luxury is extensive. For a socio-cultural approach, see Lipovetsky and Roux (2003).

[69] Paris (2006a, 382–406).

[70] Erti (1950).

CORI (produced by GFT since 1958). The sales of clothing marked with the *CORI-Biki* logo did not differ significantly from those of most other ready-to-wear companies.

The relevance of this case study lies precisely in its failure. The partnership between Biki and GFT was paradigmatic of the mutual benefits that collaboration could have brought, but they did not materialize due to the particular context within which high fashion designers and ready-to-wear companies operated. Biki certainly earned significant amounts from this agreement, and GFT leveraged her name as a marketing tool. In the 1950s, the use of specific slogans, price and size indications, as well as the characteristics of the materials used, proved to be sufficient to promote the main material features of the product (practicality, durability, affordability, and up-to-date fashion content), especially for men's clothing. However, in the following decade, different brands felt the need to consolidate and differentiate themselves. Biki's direct involvement in the promotional phase followed this direction. Nevertheless, GFT chose not to involve Biki in the management of the production process. Perhaps Biki's ideas were not as popular as expected. It is possible that the sober and conventional style of her designs, combined with the standardization typical of mass production, did not fully meet the taste of female consumers, resulting in ready-to-wear garments which, unlike their French counterparts, lacked a strong defining image. The main companies in the sector had demonstrated their ability to fully exploit the idea of mass production, but not that of fashion.[71] The same consideration applies to GFT. In its relationship with Biki, GFT prioritized standardization (economies of scale and a sizing system), clearly defining the boundary between creation and industry. This approach is evident not only in informal agreements but also in the licensing agreements signed by Biki and GFT during the 1960s.

It was only towards the end of the decade (starting from 1968 with Walter Albini) that a new generation of designers interested in establishing a closer collaboration with production partners gained prominence.[72] These figures were finally recognized for their more wide-ranging design expertise (designing the appearance and defining the 'meaning' of the

[71] Morini (2006, 317).

[72] Frisa and Tonchi (2010).

garment), which the company could leverage as an element of innovation. As we will see in the following chapters, this paradigm shift initially affected smaller and more flexible enterprises, while collaboration with larger firms was consolidated during the 1970s. This was an important transition, firstly because it contributed to the revival of the large ready-to-wear industry (including GFT).[73] Secondly, it opened the way for formalized collaborations through licensing contracts, which became a distinctive feature of the Italian fashion system in the following years.

In conclusion, it is worth mentioning that the push to improve the quality of ready-made garments also came from important high fashion designers. The motivation was the same: to expand their production range to include quality ready-to-wear and target an intermediate market segment. The outcomes were also similar. An example is the case of the Sorelle Fontana fashion house, who founded the brand *Fontana Alta Moda Pronta* (Fontana's high fashion ready-to-wear) in 1966. The brand identified mass-produced garments made by more than 400 workers in an automated system that applied American production practices using Italian Necchi sewing machines and complex patterns. The scale was far from that of GFT, and some stages of the production process (such as finishing) still followed artisanal practices. However, production exceeded 200 garments per day and aimed to further increase volumes.[74]

The experience of Sorelle Fontana came to an end in 1973, one year after the termination of the partnership between Biki and GFT. The timing is not coincidental and reflects both the previously mentioned ambivalence of the majority of Italian tailors (whose style, in a futile attempt to reconcile high fashion with the mass market, became easier but not more modern) and the paradigm shift in the organization of the production process. The Italian experience, therefore, was markedly different from that in France, where prestigious names in high fashion had, since the early twentieth century, been able to horizontally expand their offerings to include products such as accessories, perfumes, and cosmetics.[75] On the contrary, the Italian high fashion tailors, despite being established trend setters, failed to exploit their name or image in the same manner. Despite some successful experiences, therefore, even in

[73] Merlo and Perugini (2020a).

[74] Paris (2010a, 530–1).

[75] Grumbach (1993, 22–3), Grau (2000, 42–4).

the second half of the 1960s, no component of the Italian fashion supply chain was capable of managing a stable and integrated system of relations, both horizontally and vertically.

1.3 The 1970s: Italian Fashion at a Historic Turning Point

The late 1960s ushered in a period of dramatic social and economic change which included the advent of young people as a new category of consumers, women's changing role in both society and the labour market, and industrial restructuring following the 1973 oil crisis. Leaving these events in the background, this section focuses on the main actors behind the innovations that would change the history of fashion, not only Italian, i.e., the emergence of Milan as the capital of fashion.

The violent social demands, changing youth aspirations, and complex market shifts that occurred after 1968 were just the tip of the iceberg of a metamorphosis that had already begun in the previous years. In a market that was steadily diversifying and stratifying, women were playing an ever more important role, including in the area of consumption. During the 1960s, links were severed with the outdated and stereotypical female image of the past, and fashion also had to take this into account with a quantitatively and qualitatively appropriate offering. This change involved, more generally, the younger generations, who expressed their personal vision of society through the rejection of outdated consumption models. These young consumers were already spending significant sums on clothing and were seen by producers as those who would look beyond the tailored imitation of the high fashion model, instead defining and imposing new styles—clothing included. However, this scenario required new production, promotional, and distribution strategies that the Italian ready-to-wear industry was not yet fully capable of developing. There were many problems to resolve: the structure of the companies, still in transition from an artisanal to an industrial dimension; integration of the creative phase into the production process; investments in distribution; development of adequate promotional strategies; and the exploitation of new means of communication.

As we have explained in the previous sections, at the end of World War II the Italian fashion industry was still far from achieving success on an international level. Artisanal production of embroideries and accessories was well established in the country and had long been appreciated by foreign markets. However, for clothing, Italy had not yet gained the proven experience in the sector boasted by other countries—above all Germany, the UK, and the United States. The production of menswear had already taken its first steps towards standardization but, as far as women's ready-made fashion was concerned, with the exception of certain unfitted items such as raincoats, there was little fashionable alternative to made-to-measure.[76]

As a latecomer, the clothing industry in Italy developed showing the typical behaviour of a new industry still lacking a solid production and distribution structure. To make up for lost time, the organization models of foreign companies, in particular American firms, were carefully examined in order to copy and adapt them to the Italian context. Large investments were made in physical capital and technological know-how, human capital was improved, and investments were made in marketing and distribution by introducing and developing retail chains which rapidly covered at least a part of the country.[77]

Following to the oil crisis of 1973, in the mid-1970s the situation changed suddenly and a new phase began. The clothing industry went into a worldwide recession. For the leading manufacturing countries, the way out of this crisis was to delocalize production. The United States moved their production to Central America, France to North Africa, and Germany to Eastern Europe. Italy also participated in this restructuring process of the clothing industry but, unlike the foreign counterparts, delocalization involved decentralization on a domestic scale as it happened within the country. This was an obligatory choice as Italy could not count on satellite economic areas. This domestic decentralization was made possible by the widespread presence of small and medium-sized businesses, many of which had formed highly specialized manufacturing agglomerations (the so-called industrial districts).

The concept of the industrial district can be traced back to Alfred Marshall.[78] He proved that most of the advantages of large-scale production can also be achieved by a population of small-sized firms concentrated in a particular area, each specialized in different phases of production and with their labour supply in a single local market. In order

[76] White (2000, 35).

[77] Pent Fornengo (1978, 60–9), Merlo (2003b).

[78] Marshall (1920).

for the industrial district to develop, it is necessary for such a population of small businesses to be in symbiosis with the people living in the same area, possessing the appropriate social and cultural characteristics for a bottom-up process of industrialization. An industrial district, therefore, can be defined as a community of people, businesses, institutions, and associations operating in a geographically limited territory within which shared values and knowledge have been accumulated over time. The high level of productive specialization, together with a number of equally important cultural, social, and institutional variables, characterizes the industrial district. The combination of these variables which often, although not necessarily, includes a well-established tradition of craftsmanship, contributes to the generation of economies of agglomeration that are external to the firms but internal to the geographical area. They are the ingredients of the Marshallian 'industrial atmosphere' which is felt within the district. An atmosphere imbued with a widespread sense of belonging to the district that is derived from the involvement of the entire community in the productive activity and from family and trust-based relationships that facilitate the flow of information and make access to financial resources easier.

In other words, the industrial district differs from other forms of network organization because it possesses a common collective identity shared by local actors and rooted in a unique social and cultural context. This collective identity is an intangible resource that helps to break down communication barriers, reduces costs associated with building specialized productive relationships, and facilitates the creation of learning networks among local entrepreneurs. However, not all types of production processes are suitable to provide the technical conditions required for the particular form of symbiosis between production activity and community life that characterizes the industrial district. Production processes that can be carried out successfully in the district must have special features, such as divisibility into phases and the possibility of moving the products of each phase products in space and time. These technological features allow a highly detailed division of labour, which allows all members of the industrial district to contribute to the overall social process of production.

Industrial districts emerged in the 1970s as the distinctive characteristic of the Italian industry. Correspondingly, academic literature dealing with them boomed, providing empirical evidence of their prominent attributes.[79] Whether newly formed or with long-standing histories, they are all characterized by high specialization, strong propensity for innovation and cooperation between businesses which guarantees the advantages—in terms of economy of scale—of large-scale production, while preserving the unique flexibility of small firms, along with their ability to swiftly adapt to changes in demand. Not surprisingly, the textile, clothing, and accessory industries, particularly footwear, are among those that have thrived the most within industrial districts. In these industries, the optimal size of firms in terms of economies of scale is smaller than in capital-intensive industries, making small incremental innovations more crucial than disruptive inventions, and where the contribution of creative design can make a difference in achieving or maintaining a competitive advantage.[80] These peculiarities became even more decisive in the 1970s, a decade in which the final demand began to be constantly affected by changes in both the national and the international markets, not to mention increasingly fickle fashion trends.

Interestingly, textile, clothing, and accessories are the industries in which the greatest number of industrial districts have survived. In 2011, 141 Italian manufacturing areas could be classified as industrial districts. The majority of them (130) have been classified as Made in Italy industrial districts. Textiles and clothing (22.7%), personal goods (17.0%), and leather and footwear (12.1%) made up approximately 22, 17, and 12% of the total, respectively.[81] These figures are even more interesting considering that, starting in the final years of the twentieth century, international competition has forced industrial districts to change dramatically,[82] to the point that the concept of industrial districts and vertically integrated large-scale firms as alternative development models has been questioned.[83]

[79] Fuà and Zacchia (1983) were among the first comprehensive review of the topic that continued to be debated until the early 2000s. See Becattini, Bellandi and De Propris (2011).

[80] Becattini (1979).

[81] ISTAT (2015).

[82] Rabellotti, Carabelli and Hirsch (2009).

[83] Lazerson and Lorenzoni (1999).

In terms of territorial distribution, with few exceptions, industrial districts developed more in regions where the process of industrialization proceeded at a faster and more intense pace following World War II. It is therefore plausible that industrial districts, at least those newly formed at the time, were born from the dismantling or reorganization of existing larger firms into smaller production units. Available figures seem to confirm this hypothesis. They show that the Italian clothing industry emerged from the crisis of the 1970s completely transformed. Between 1971 and 1981, the number of firms with fewer than 500 employees increased by nearly 140,000, 113,000 of which were small firms with fewer than ten workers. As far as employment is concerned, the small firms set up in that decade created more than 100,000 new jobs while the large companies lost about 80,000 jobs. At the beginning of the 1980s, nearly 90% of jobs in the Italian clothing industry were in companies with fewer than 100 employees.[84] Such impressive figures show that the way out of the recession of the 1970s was achieved primarily by firms downsizing, that is, through the de-verticalization and decentralization of production. However, Italian clothing companies also introduced a wide range of new labour-saving technologies. Technical progress included sophisticated computer-assisted design (CAD) systems for the pre-assembly stages such as pattern grading, lay planning and pattern modification, computer-controlled cutting systems, and operator-programmable sewing machines—versatile equipment able to cope easily with changes in fashion.[85]

It is undeniable that labour-saving technologies and downsizing strategies were both aimed at reducing production costs. However, since the decentralization process took place within the country it achieved objectives beyond cost reduction, the rise in which was one of the factors that led to the recession. Thanks to decentralization, the Italian clothing industry continued to pursue flexibility, enabling it to manage complex production processes through networked production units deeply rooted in diverse local cultures and traditions, all centred around labour, expertise, and the product. For the first time in its (short) history, the Italian clothing industry could boast a competitive advantage made stronger

[84] Pent Fornengo (1992, 216), Frey et al. (1979).

[85] For a more detailed analysis of costs and benefits entailed by the new technologies listed above see Pent Fornengo (1992, 213).

by the nature of the crisis which hit the sector in those years. In fact, firms manufacturing clothing—and particularly the largest vertically integrated businesses—had to manage a crisis fuelled by rising labour and raw material costs but, at the same time, they also had to face a broader process which changed the prevailing model of consumption. On the demand side, a new type of consumer was emerging—young people—who demanded new, more informal, and less traditional fashions. It was young people who first rejected mass-produced industrial clothing, and it was young people who gave the first push towards the differentiation of clothes which was to become part of a new system of symbols strongly opposed to the conformity of adult living (and dressing). Starting from the 1970s, clothing for young people became an autonomous and rapidly growing market. This market required greater segmentation of supply and the development of different styles.

On the supply side, alongside French designers, new competitors were emerging on the international stage, particularly from America. Among them, well-known fashion designers such as Calvin Klein, Donna Karan, and Ralph Lauren,[86] began to attract an international clientele and, by the mid-1970s, their names were synonymous with contemporary American style in which casual yet elegant separates remained a distinctive feature. Soon, these designers recognized the commercial potential of producing fashion collections which were more accessible than *haute couture*, and as a result, they quickly evolved from individual designers to establishing large fashion companies and managed to penetrate international markets.

Thus, during the 1970s the clothing industry was preparing to turn its back on the era of standardized clothing manufacture, which had introduced classic and elaborate garments into the wardrobes of consumers, and instead advance with the production of clothing in a wide and ever-changing variety of styles and colours. Although flexibility, a key feature of small and medium-sized enterprises, meant Italian clothing firms were ready to cater for the new way of dressing and consumption, the new business model adopted during those years aimed to go further than simply exploiting its ability to adapt to changes in demand. Rather, companies invested in a new type of human capital—fashion designers—with whom collaborations were born not merely to follow new trends in taste and consumption but rather to anticipate them, to predict them at least

[86] McDowell (2005), Gaines and Churcher (1994), Sischy (2006).

one season in advance, thus aligning with the timelines involved in the planning of industrial production.

Collaborative relationships between fashion and industry have, at times, radically changed the course of the history of the companies involved. The case of Callaghan provides evidence of the irreversible turning point caused by incorporating stylistic creativity into a company whose products were far from being subject to fashion dictates.[87] The name Callaghan was born in 1966 as a brand for a line of products by the Zamasport company, which had a long history in the production of underwear. In 1924, Augusto and Giacinto Zanetti founded the Maglificio Zanetti. In the mid-1950s, the brothers decided to each have their own separate business. Augusto founded ZAMA and introduced the production of sportswear and cotton jersey sweaters for ladies and men, in addition to underwear. While these innovations showed a keen awareness of signals of change in what consumers were buying and their lifestyles, they were still anchored to a type of clothing that was not yet subject to the rapid changes of fashion. Only a decade later, when the second generation took over management of the business, did fashion begin to guide the production lines. Patterned jersey shirts were produced in addition to cotton sweaters and in cotton interlock T-shirts in addition to vests. The *ZAMA* brand, which had until then been used to label all the factory's production, was replaced with the 'C' for Callaghan in a repeated decorative design on the fabrics. However, it was only in 1968 when collaboration began with Walter Albini that "for the first-time designer and company met at operational level to discuss a product as particular as knitwear, considered by many to be the Cinderella of fashion fabrics, the outcast in a stylish wardrobe, the neglected article in an elitist market".[88] This partnership changed the history of the company, which was well prepared in the 1970s to confront the crisis and new market trends. From the mid-1970s, designers such as Norma Kamali, Helmut Lang, Luciano Soprani, Romeo Gigli, and Gianni Versace collaborated with Callaghan. Furthermore, Callaghan was one of the producers (alongside Basile, Escargots, Misterfox, and Diamant's, and shortly thereafter Sportmax) specializing in different yet complementary products (jackets, knitwear, jerseys, jumpsuits, shirts) that participated in the fashion show held in

[87] Giordani Aragno (1997).

[88] On Italian knitwear see Belfanti (2005, 105–50).

Milan, where Walter Albini presented the collection he had designed for them.

Although the collaborative relationship between the fashion designer and textile and clothing companies was primarily a way out of the crisis that had ended the Italian 'golden age', its impact went beyond the peculiar economic circumstances of the 1970s. The Italian fashion system was enriched by a combination of experiences, relationships, and knowledge that resulted not only in a closer and continuous collaboration between fashion and industry. Fashion designers had the opportunity to engage with the business world before becoming entrepreneurs themselves in the realms of creativity and taste. On the other hand, the clothing industry, thanks to fashion designers, began to create and guide fashion trends. As a result, product innovation, rather than the characteristics of organizational and distributional innovation typical of vertical integration processes, became the focal point of the clothing business.

Significantly, a large company, more precisely one of the largest Italian clothing companies, provides the most convincing evidence that the 1970s was a historical turning point for Italian fashion. As explained in the previous section, GFT was at the forefront of experimentation with collaboration between high fashion designers. Although ultimately unsuccessful, the partnership between GFT and Biki had paved the way for collaborations based on the recognition that an insurmountable divide separated the fashion designer's know-how from the manufacturer's capabilities. Producers had to unconditionally accept their partner's designs decisions, while fashion designers had no say in the manufacturing process. In this respect, the collaboration with Biki differed significantly from that experienced by GFT with prominent fashion designers from the beginning of the 1970s. In reality, the collaboration with Biki was established when GFT was focused on turning itself into a highly efficient producer of standardized men's clothing. Its production system was extremely rigid, and the company's capacity to produce in high volume was aimed at minimizing unit costs. Female consumers still represented only a residual market catered for by GFT, especially when compared to the emerging mass market for men's clothing in Italy.

By the end of the 1960s, however, massive labour unrest throughout Italy made the company's position as a low-cost producer difficult to sustain. In this context, GFT turned to alliances with fashion designers to aggressively address the market, rather than merely defending itself against fierce competition. The company aimed to expand its product line by entering high-end niche markets, rather than catering solely to the emerging mass market. It sought to capitalize on the growing demand for women's wear and sportswear, instead of focusing solely on the production of men's clothing. Ultimately, this transformation shifted the company's orientation from a production-driven business to a designer-oriented enterprise.

Emanuel Ungaro was the first fashion designer to collaborate in implementing the new strategy. The son of an Italian tailor, Ungaro trained at Cristóbal Balenciaga's atelier before launching his own fashion house in 1965. Along with Pierre Cardin and André Courrèges, who had also been nurtured in Balenciaga studio during the 1950s, Ungaro played an important role in the rejuvenation of Parisian fashion. When GFT hired him in 1971, he was already well known as a fashion designer who created not only elegant but also bold and provocative feminine looks.

Significantly, with respect to the legal aspects of the licensing contract, GFT was not directly involved in the partnership with Emanuel Ungaro. A new company, CIDAT (*Compagnia Italiana di Abbigliamento Torino*) was created specifically to manage the relationship with the fashion designer. Over time, this partnership gave rise to collections such as Ungaro Parallèle (luxury ready-to-wear), Ungaro Solodonna (ready-to-wear), Ungaro Ter (so-called diffusion line, more accessible than the *prêt-à-porter* lines), and Ungaro Uomo (men's clothing), with no mention of the manufacturer's name.

A partnership with a nonconformist French designer, a more sophisticated corporate structure, renewed contractual obligations, along with patronymic collections, all can be considered signs that a new entrepreneurial attitude was emerging in both the fashion designer and the clothing manufacturer. For the former, economies of scale, managerial capabilities, retailing, marketing, and advertising skills were within reach. For the latter, the era of uniformity was over. Clothing, which had been produced to cater to the homogenization of mass consumption in the 1960s, was reinvented to increasingly emphasize differentiation within mass production. Since the early 1970s, the Italian clothing industry had become aware of the enormous economic potential of fashion in terms of creating market opportunities, stimulating a continuous flow of new needs, planning product obsolescence, and educating consumers to be increasingly discerning. For large companies, the time had finally come for them to transform into a fundamental pillar of the Italian fashion system.

The late 1970s marked the second and most important phase of GFT's evolution as an industrial fashion company. It began with the establishment of partnerships with two well-known Italian fashion designers, Giorgio Armani and Valentino Garavani, who signed agreements with GFT in 1978 and 1979, respectively.[89] In 1957, Armani worked at La Rinascente, before joining Cerruti, one of Italy's largest producers of men's clothing, as a stylist. With the encouragement of his friend Sergio Galeotti, Armani then started to collaborate as a freelance designer with other companies. In 1975, Armani and Galeotti founded Giorgio Armani Spa. The company's first collection—a men's clothing line—debuted that year. In 1976, Armani launched a women's collection which received a warm reception. Since then, Armani's collections have been included among the foreign luxury goods sold by Barneys, the famous New York department store. In the case of Armani, the licensing agreement covered both the Giorgio Armani *white label* diffusion (or bridge) line—a secondary line intended to reach customers with lower price points—and the more exclusive Giorgio Armani *black label* collection. In 1979, GFT and Armani created a joint venture in the United States (the Giorgio Armani Men's Wear Corporation), which introduced Armani's labels to a wider North American audience.

Valentino founded his atelier in Rome in 1959, after studying in Paris and training as an apprentice under Jean Dessès and Guy Laroche. In 1969, he opened his first ready-to-wear boutique and introduced the 'V' logo. Valentino's emblem owed much of its initial success to the American customers, who were particularly appreciative of his soft tailoring and lavish evening gowns. Throughout the 1960s and 1970s, his glamorous, sophisticated designs attracted high-profile customers such as Jacqueline Onassis, Elizabeth Taylor, and the Empress of Iran, Farah Diba.[90]

GFT's goal was to create fashionable ready-to-wear garments by combining the advantages of industrial production in terms of scale, with those derived from the creative control of an iconic fashion designer, which conveyed a sense of independence, uniqueness, and authentic brand identity.[91] In her extensive research into the Italian design revolution, Silvia Giacomoni observed that, in the second half of the 1970s,

[89] Merlo and Perugini (2020a).

[90] Mendes and De la Haye, (1999, 204).

[91] Potvin (2019, 85).

Italians "lost their accent". A new 'Italian look' emerged, which was built upon renowned capabilities in manufacturing high-quality textiles and fashion goods—together with the outstanding talents of a new generation of fashion designers.[92]

These partnerships allowed both GFT and designers to seize the opportunities offered by the growing interest in Italian fashion in the American market. As highlighted by the art historian John Potvin, it was not until the deal with GFT that the Armani brand became a cultural and economic force to be reckoned with outside of Italy. Since his debut under his own name in 1975, the designer had received great acclaim, but his access to American customers was still rather limited. The huge commercial success of the new diffusion line allowed him to expand his influence within the highly lucrative American market. Thanks to the industrial partnership with GFT, Armani's diffusion line retained many distinctive features of the designer's style—that "very classic, elegant, relaxed and truly Italian" style—despite being sold at half the price of the *black label* couture collection.[93]

If the birth of Italian fashion conventionally dates back to the early 1950s, the birth of the Italian fashion industry is deeply rooted in the 1970s. The configuration of the industry that emerged in response to the changes occurring in national and international markets provided the backbone of the ensuing development of the fashion industry. Companies agglomerated in industrial districts were crucial to diversification into a wide variety of products, including leather accessories, shoes, jewellery, knitwear, buttons, and so on. These businesses were also crucial as developers of new materials such as luxury yarns. The largest firms played a crucial role in transforming mass production into fashion through industrial design.

The changes in the national and international markets also fuelled competition among the Italian fashion capitals. The city that fully exploited the new opportunities offered by the decline of Paris and the emergence of the United States as a reference model could finally aspire to achieve the status of *the* Italian capital of Italian fashion. It was Milan which won the competition. Milan began to rival Florence as a fashion capital starting from the early 1970s, when several fashion

[92] Giacomoni (1984, 9).

[93] Potvin (2019, 284).

creators, including Walter Albini, abandoned the Florentine shows to present their collections in Milan, producing a change similar that caused by the first Giorgini fashion show in 1951. Within a decade, Milan had become the international capital of *prêt-à-porter*. In 1979, three complementary events would make up Milan fashion week. Firstly, there was *Milano Collezioni*, the major show where the most important designers would present their collections. The second event was *Milanovendemoda*, a fashion trade fair founded in 1968. Finally, there was *Modit*, a *prêt-à-porter* show which was centred on the link between fashion and industry.

The reasons for Milan's eventual emergence as *the* Italian capital of fashion are strongly related to the variety and specialization of resources accumulated in the Milanese urban area as well as to the institutional intermediaries working within it.[94] How they reacted to the exogenous shock of World War II on the world of fashion, and how they were equipped to respond to the changes on the demand side are key questions.

In summary, Italian ready-to-wear was born in an extremely turbulent context, while markets were shaken by deep and irreversible changes in supply and demand trends which required the adoption of new business models. Indeed, at the beginning of the 1980s, the strengths of Italian fashion—mainly product quality, style, and prices—continued to be competitive advantages but marketing strategies became more critical than ever for successful competition, and branding with the name of the designer became the core business of the marketing strategy pursued by Italian clothing companies.

Following Milan's rise to international prominence in ready-to-wear fashion, at the expense of the previously leading centres in Rome and Florence, a new generation of designers emerged. This was not simply a generational change. As the reader shall see in the following chapters, the generational change coincided with a shift in the nature of fashion itself. Fashion became no longer a matter of diffusion of clothes, accessories, and such, but rather evolved into the process that organizes the emergence and demise of trends, providing producers with an array of stylistic options in a given place and time. How did all these changes affect the Italian fashion system? The next chapter charts the main organizations involved in the management of the Italian fashion from the 1950s to

[94] Merlo and Polese (2006).

the 1970s, focusing mainly on their organizational structure and activities. The institutional dynamics that led to the consolidation of the Italian fashion system during the 1980s will be explained in the third chapter.

References

AIIA. 1980. *L'industria italiana degli impermeabili* [Biblioteca Bovisa Candiani del Politecnico di Milano, sez. Tremelloni (3 MAG EC.02.0391)].

AIIA. 1985. *Quarant'anni di abbigliamento: 1945–1985*. Milan: AIIA.

Amatori, Franco. 1989. *La Rinascente. Proprietà e direzione 1917–1969*. Milan: Franco Angeli.

Bairati, Piero. 1986. *Sul filo di lana. Cinque generazioni di imprenditori: i Marzotto*. Bologna: Mulino.

Becattini, Giacomo, Marco Bellandi and Lisa De Propris. 2011. "Industrial Districts: The Contemporary Debate." *Economia e Politica Industriale—Journal of Industrial and Business Economics* 38 (3): 53–75.

Becattini, Giacomo. 1979. "Dal 'settore' industriale al 'distretto' industriale. Alcune riflessioni sull'unità di indagine dell'economia industriale." *Rivista di Economia e Politica Industriale* 5 (1): 7–21.

Belfanti, Carlo Marco. 2005. *Calze e maglie. Moda e innovazione nell'industria italiana della maglieria dal Rinascimento a oggi*. Mantua: Tre Lune.

Belfanti, Carlo Marco. 2008. *Civiltà della moda*. Bologna: Mulino.

Belfanti, Carlo Marco. 2015. "Renaissance and 'Made in Italy': Marketing Italian Fashion through History (1949–1952)." *Journal of Modern Italian Studies* 20 (1): 53–66.

Blaszczyk, Regina Lee. 2007. "Du Pont de Nemours: mode et révolution des textiles synthétiques." In *La mode des Sixties. L'entreé dans la modernité*, edited by D. Veillon and M. Ruffat, 202–19. Paris: Autrement.

Blignaut, Hélène. 1995. *La scala di vetro. Il romanzo della vita di Biki*. Milan: Rusconi.

Boneschi, Marta. 2014. "Da pioniera della moda a militante pacifista. Rosa Genoni." In *Donne nella Grande Guerra,* edited by M. Boneschi et al., 207–20. Bologna: Mulino.

Bossaglia, Rossana, Ezio Godoli, and Marco Rosci, eds. 1994. *Torino 1902. Le arti decorative internazionali del nuovo secolo*. Milan: Fabbri.

Bottero, Amelia. 1969. "Democrazia del lusso." *L'Abbigliamento Italiano* 10 (July): 5–6.

Bottero, Amelia. 1979. *Nostra signora la moda*. Milan: Mursia.

Brunetti, Giorgio, and Arnaldo Camuffo. 1994. *Marzotto. Continuità e sviluppo*. Turin: Isedi.

Calanca, Daniela, and Simona Segre Reinach. 2021. "Rethinking Fashion Brands in The Era of Digital Media." *Zone Mode Journal* 11 (1): 1.

Capalbi, Franca. 1961. “13° Samia torinese.” *Linea. Rivista dell’alta moda*, Winter Edition.

Capalbo, Cinzia. 2012. *Storia della moda a Roma. Sarti, culture e stili di una capitale dal 1871 a oggi*. Rome: Donzelli.

Capuzzo, Paolo, ed. 2003. *Genere, generazione e consumi. L’Italia degli anni Sessanta*. Rome: Carocci.

Carrarini, Rita. 2003. “La stampa di moda dall’Unità ad oggi.” In *Storia d’Italia, Annali 19. La moda* edited by C.M. Belfanti and F. Giusberti, 797–833. Turin: Einaudi.

Cerretano, Valerio. 2022. “Autarky, Market Creation and Innovation: Snia Viscosa and Saici, 1933–1970.” *Business History* 64 (6): 1110–30.

Ciabattoni, Amos. 1976. *Il sistema moda*. Turin: Editoriale Valentino.

Colli, Andrea. 2003. “Fibre chimiche.” In *Storia d’Italia, Annali 19. La moda* edited by C. M. Belfanti and F. Giusberti, 483–522. Turin: Einaudi.

Comitato Italiano per il Cotone. 1960. *Il mercato degli impermeabili: osservazioni raccolte in interviste condotte presso industriali della confezione* [Biblioteca Bovisa Candiani del Politecnico di Milano, sez. Tremelloni, (3 MAG EC.02.0211)].

Italiana, Confederazione Generale dell’Industria. 1958. *Annuario*. Rome: Confindustria.

Cunningham, Patricia A., and Linda Welters, eds. 2005. *Twentieth-Century American Fashion*. Oxford: Berg.

Davanzo Poli, Doretta. 2003. “Il sarto.” In *Storia d’Italia, Annali 19. La moda* edited by C.M. Belfanti and F. Giusberti, 523–60. Turin: Einaudi.

De Grazia, Victoria. 2005. *Irresistible Empire. America’s Advance through Twentieth-Century Europe*. Cambridge: Belknap.

De Guttry, Maria Paola Irene, Gloria Raimondi Maino, and Gabriella Tarquini, eds. 2018. *Maria Monaci Gallenga: Arte e moda tra le due guerre*. Rome: Palombi.

De Spigliati, Riccardo. 1902. *Guida della prima esposizione internazionale d’arte decorativa moderna*. Turin: Tipografia Matteo Artale.

English, Bonnie. 2007. *A Cultural History of Fashion in the 20th Century*. Oxford-New York: Berg.

Erti. 1950. “Le sorprese di Biky.” *Grazia*, 8th April.

Erti. 1952. “Questa la moda che entusiasma l’America.” *Grazia*, 6th September.

Fauri, Francesca. 2010. *Il Piano Marshall e l’Italia*. Bologna: Mulino.

Felice, Emanuele, and Giovanni Vecchi. 2015. “Italy’s Growth and Decline, 1861–2011.” *Journal of Interdisciplinary History* 45 (4): 507–48.

Fenoaltea, Stefano. 1998. “The Growth of Italy’s Silk Industry, 1861–1913: A Statistical Reconstruction”. *Rivista di Storia Economica* 16 (2): 119–46.

Fenoaltea, Stefano. 2000. “The Growth of Italy’s Wool Industry, 1861–1913: A Statistical Reconstruction.” *Rivista di Storia Economica* 17 (2): 139–72.

Fenoaltea, Stefano. 2001. "The Growth of Italy's Cotton Industry, 1861–1913: A Statistical Reconstruction." *Rivista di Storia Economica* 5 (special issue) (3): 275–318.

Fenoaltea, Stefano. 2002. "Textile Production in Italy, 1861–1913". *Rivista di Storia Economica* 18 (1): 3–40.

Fiorentini Capitani, Aurora. 1991. *Moda italiana anni Cinquanta e Sessanta*. Florence: Cantini.

Fiorentini Capitani, Aurora. 1996. "L'ornamento di 'pura arte italiana': la moda di Rosa Genoni." In *Abiti in festa: l'ornamento e la sartoria italiana* edited by C. Chiarelli, 40–59. Livorno: Sillabe.

Fratini, Francesca, ed. 1971. *Torino 1902: Polemiche in Italia sull'Arte Nuova*. Turin: Martano.

Frey, Luigi, Renata Livraghi and Pino Lucà Trombetta. 1979. *Occupazione e ristrutturazioni industriali. Il caso del tessile abbigliamento*. Milan: Franco Angeli.

Frisa, Maria Luisa, Stefano Tonchi. 2010. *Walter Albini and His Times. All Power to the Imagination*. Venice: Marsilio.

Fuà, Giorgio, and Carlo Zacchia, eds. 1983. *Industrializzazione senza fratture*. Bologna: Mulino.

Gaines, Steven, and Sharon Churcher. 1994. *Obsession: The Lives and Times of Calvin Klein*. New York: Carol Publishing Group.

Gamberini, Giorgio. 1957. "Profilo della struttura della distribuzione tessile." In *Il problema tessile italiano*. Vol. II *La distribuzione tessile e la stagionalità nel settore tessile* edited by Comitato nazionale per la produttività, Gruppo di lavoro per il settore tessile. Rome: A.B.E.T.E.

Giacomoni, Silvia. 1984. *The Italian Look Reflected*. Milan: Mazzotta.

Giordani Aragno, Bonizza. 1997. *Callaghan, 1966. La nascita del prêt-à-porter italiano*. Milan: Mazzotta.

Gnoli, Sofia. 2000. *La donna, l'eleganza, il fascismo: la moda italiana dalle origini all'Ente nazionale della moda*. Catania: Edizioni del Prisma.

Gnoli, Sofia. 2005. *Un secolo di moda italiana (1900–2000)*. Rome: Meltemi.

Grau, Francoise Marie. 2000. *La haute couture*. Paris: PUF.

Grumbach, Didier. 1993. *Histoires de la mode*. Paris: Seuil.

Handley, Susannah. 1999. *Nylon: The Story of a Fashion Revolution*. London: Bloomsbury.

Heynold Von Graefe, Blida. 1962. "Le vetrine trascurate." *L'Abbigliamento Italiano* 4 (November-December): 20–21.

ISTAT. 2015. *9° Censimento generale dell'industria e dei servizi e censimento delle istituzioni non profit. I distretti industriali 2011*. Rome: Istat.

Jones, Geoffrey, and Véronique Pouillard. 2013. *Christian Dior: A New Look for Haute Couture*. Cambridge, MA: Harvard Business School (HBS case no. 9–809–159).

Kawamura, Yuniya. 2005. *Fashion-Ology. An Introduction to Fashion Studies*. Oxford: Berg.
Kipping, Matthias, and Ove Bjarnar, eds. 1998. *The Americanisation of European Business: The Marshall Plan and the Transfer of US Management Models*. London: Routledge.
L'Abbigliamento Italiano. 1960. "Un'importante collaborazione italo-tedesca." *L'Abbigliamento Italiano* 2 (June): 2.
L'Abbigliamento Italiano. 1961a. "Aperto il nuovo reparto 'Cori' del negozio Marus in via Roma a Torino." *L'Abbigliamento Italiano* 3 (October): 24.
L'Abbigliamento Italiano. 1961b. "Normalizzazione delle taglie e difetti dei tessuti impiegati nella confezione." *L'Abbigliamento Italiano* 3 (November-December): 18.
L'Abbigliamento Italiano. 1965. "La moda e l'eleganza nell'abbigliamento sono più importanti del prezzo." *L'Abbigliamento Italiano* 7 (August): 13.
Lazerson, Mark H., and Gianni Lorenzoni. 1999. "The Firms That Feed Industrial Districts: A Return to the Italian Source." *Industrial & Corporate Change* 8 (2): 235–66.
Lees-Maffei, Grace, and Kjetil Fallan, eds. 2014. *Made in Italy: Rethinking a Century of Italian Design*. London: Bloomsbury.
Levra, Umberto, and Rosanna Roccia, eds. 2003. *Le Esposizioni torinesi 1805–1911. Specchio del progresso e macchina del consenso*. Turin: Archivio storico.
Lipovetsky, Gilles and Elyette Roux. 2003. *Le luxe éternel. De l'âge du sacré au temps des marques*. Paris: Gallimard.
Lipovetsky, Gilles. 1987. *L'empire de l'éphèmere*. Paris: Gallimard.
Lupano, Mario, and Alessandra Vaccari, eds. 2009. *Fashion at the Time of Fascism: Italian Modern Lifestyle in the 1920s–1930s*. Bologna: Damiani.
Marcucci, Raffaella. 2004. *Anibo e Made in Italy. Storia dei buying offices in Italia*. Florence: Vallecchi.
Marshall, Alfred. 1920. *Principles of Economics*. London: Macmillan.
Masiola, Rosanna, and Sabrina Cittadini. 2020. *The Golden Dawn of Italian Fashion: A Cross Cultural Perspective on Maria Monaci Gallenga*. Newcastle upon Tyne, UK: Cambridge Scholars Publishing.
McDowell, Colin. 2005. *Ralph Lauren: The Man, the Vision, the Style*. London: Cassell Illustrated.
Mendes, Valerie, and Amy de la Haye. 1999. *20th Century Fashion*. London: Thames and Hudson.
Merlo, Elisabetta, and Francesca Polese. 2006. "Turning Fashion into Business. The Emergence of Milan as an International Fashion Hub." *Business History* 80 (3): 415–47.
Merlo, Elisabetta, and Mario Perugini. 2020a. "Making Italian fashion global: Brand building and management at Gruppo Finanziario Tessile (1950s–1990s)." *Business History* 62 (1): 42–69.

Merlo, Elisabetta, and Mario Perugini. 2020b. "The Determinants of the Emergence of Turin as the First Capital of Italian Fashion Industry (1900–1960)." *Fashion Theory* 24 (3): 325–48.
Merlo, Elisabetta. 2003a. "*Le origini del sistema moda*," In *Storia d'Italia, Annali 19*. In *La moda*, edited by C. M. Belfanti and F. Giusberti, 667–97. Turin: Einaudi.
Merlo, Elisabetta. 2003b. *Moda italiana. Storia di un'industria dall'Ottocento a oggi*. Venice: Marsilio.
Merlo, Elisabetta. 2014. "When fashion met industry. Biki and Gruppo Finanziario Tessile (1957–72)." *Journal of Modern Italian Studies* 20 (1): 92–110.
Merlo, Elisabetta. 2015. "Size Revolution: The Industrial Foundation of the Italian Clothing Business." *Business History* 57 (6): 919–94.
Merlo, Elisabetta. 2021. "Fashion: Production, Commercialisation, and Consumption." In *Leading Economic Risorgimento. Lombardy in the 19th Century* edited by S. Conca Messina, 178–95. London: Routledge.
Mingardo, Mirella. 2013. "Rosa Genoni, tra moda e impegno politico." *Storia in Lombardia* 33 (2): 149–79.
Misiano, Francesca. 2014. "L'Esposizione del Sempione 1906. Milano in vetrina." *Diacronie* [Online] 18 (2).
Morini, Enrica. 2005. "La semplice, meravigliosa moda italiana." In *Anni Cinquanta, la nascita della creatività italiana*, 266–307. Florence: Artificio Skira.
Morini, Enrica. 2006. *Storia della moda XVIII-XX secolo*. Milan: Skyra.
Morris, Jonathan. 1998. "The Fascist 'Disciplining' of the Italian Retail Sector, 1922–40." *Business History* 40 (4): 138–64.
Morris, Jonathan. 1999. "Contesting Retail Space in Italy: Competition and Corporatism 1915–60." *The International Review of Retail, Distribution and Consumer Research* 9 (3): 291–306.
Morris, Jonathan. 2003. "Le vetrine della moda." In *La Moda. Storia d'Italia. Annali 19* edited by C. M. Belfanti and F. Giusberti, 835–67. Turin: Einaudi.
Pagani, Elisabetta, and Rosanna Pavoni. 1987. "La confezione negli anni Sessanta tra crisi ed innovazione." In *La moda italiana*, vol. II *Dall'antimoda allo stilismo* edited by G. Buttazzi and A. Mottola Molfino, 32–43. Milan: Electa.
Palmer, Alexandra. 2009. *Dior: A New Look, a New Enterprise 1947–57*. London: Victoria & Albert Museum.
Papadia, Elena. 2005. *La Rinascente*. Bologna: Mulino.
Paris, Ivan. 2006a. *Oggetti cuciti. L'abbigliamento pronto in Italia dal primo dopoguerra agli anni Settanta*. Milan: Franco Angeli.
Paris, Ivan. 2006b. "'Industrie di confezione a serie'. La produzione italiana di abiti pronti tra le due guerre." *Società e Storia* 113 (3): 519–58.

Paris, Ivan. 2010a. "Fashion as a System. Changes in Demand as the Basis for the Establishment of the Italian Fashion System (1960–1970)." *Enterprise & Society* 11 (3): 524–59.

Paris, Ivan. 2010b. "Orígenes del Made in Italy. Moda italiana y mercado internacional en la segunda posguerra (1951–1969)." *Revista de Historia Industrial* 19 (42): 121–55.

Paulicelli, Eugenia. 2004. *Fashion under Fascism: Beyond the Black Shirt*. Oxford—New York: Berg.

Paulicelli, Eugenia. 2017. *Rosa Genoni. La moda è una cosa seria. Milano Expo 1906 e la Grande Guerra*. Milan: Deleyva.

Pent Fornengo, Graziella. 1978. *L'industria italiana dell'abbigliamento*. Bologna: Mulino.

Pent Fornengo, Graziella. 1992. "Product Differentiation and Process Innovation in the Italian Clothing Industry." In *Industry on the Move: Causes and Consequences of International Relocation in the Manufacturing Industry*, edited by Van Liemt, Gustav, 209–33. Geneva: International Labour Office.

Piazzoni, Irene. 1995. "Milano e le esposizioni universali (1860–1900)." In *Innovazione e modernizzazione in Italia fra Otto e Novecento*, edited by E. Decleva, C.G. Lacaita, and A. Ventura, 529–77. Milan: Franco Angeli.

Pinchera, Valeria, and Diego Rinallo. 2020. "The Emergence of Italy as a Fashion Country: Nation Branding and Collective Meaning Creation at Florence's Fashion Shows (1951–1965)." *Business History* 62 (1): 151–78.

Pinchera, Valeria. 2009. *La moda in Italia e in Toscana. Dalle origini alla globalizzazione*. Venice: Marsilio.

Potvin, John. 2019. *Giorgio Armani: The Milanese Tailor of Elegance*. London: Bloomsbury Publishing Plc.

Pouillard, Véronique. 2021. "Keeping Designs and Brands Authentic: The Resurgence of the Post-war. French Fashion Business under the Challenge of US Mass Production." *European Review of History* 20 (5): 815–35.

Rabellotti, Roberta, Anna Carabelli, and Giovanna Hirsch. 2009. "Italian Industrial Districts on the Move: Where Are They Going?" *European Planning Studies* 17 (1): 19–41.

Rasi, Giuseppe. 1959. "Rivelazioni di un'inchiesta: sono 8 milioni le gonne estive vendute in Italia." *L'Abbigliamento Italiano* 1 (December): 8.

Redondi, Pietro, and Paola Zocchi, eds. 2006. *Milano 1906. L'Esposizione internazionale del Sempione. La scienza, la città, la vita*. Milan: Guerini e Associati.

Repek, Claudio, ed. 2003. *La confezione di un sogno: Storia delle donne della Lebole*. Rome: Ediesse.

Robiola, Elsa. 1951. "La linea e i suoi dettagli." *Bellezza*, September.

Rossetti, Elsa. 1961. "Presentazioni. Apem." *L'Abbigliamento Italiano* 3 (July-August): 25.

Rossetti, Elsa. 1963. "Inaugurato a Settimo Torinese il più grande stabilimento d'Europa di confezioni maschili." *L'Abbigliamento Italiano* 5 (September-October): 21.

Roverato, Giorgio. 1986. *I Marzotto: Una casa industriale*. Milan: Franco Angeli.

Savi, Lucia. 2023. *A New History of 'Made in Italy': Fashion and Textiles in Post-War Italy*. London: Bloomsbury Visual Arts.

Scarpellini, Emanuela. 2011. *Material Nation. A Consumer History of Modern Italy*. Oxford: Oxford University Press.

Schröter. Harm G. 2005. *Americanization of the European Economy: A Compact Survey of American Economic Influence in Europe Since the 1880s*. Dordrecht: Springer.

Settimi, Bruno. 1964. *L'abitificio moderno*. Milan: La Moda Maschile.

Settimi, Bruno. 1970. "Il semicalibrato." *L'Abbigliamento Italiano* 11 (December): 27.

Settimi, Bruno. 1971a. "Il semicalibrato anglo-americano." *L'Abbigliamento Italiano* 12 (January): 14.

Settimi, Bruno. 1971b. "Il calibrato americano." *L'Abbigliamento Italiano* 12 (February): 18–19.

Sischy, Ingrid. 2006. *DonnaKaran*. New York: Assouline.

Soyer, Daniel, ed. 2005. *A Coat of Many Colors: Immigration, Globalization, and Reform in New York City's Garment Industry*. New York: Fordham University Press.

Stanfill, Sonnet. 2014. *Italian Style. Fashion Since 1945*. London: Victoria & Albert Pubns.

Stanfill, Sonnet. 2015. "The Role of the *sartoria* in Post-war Italy." *Journal of Modern Italian Studies* 20 (1): 83–91.

Stanfill, Sonnet. 2018. "Anonymous Tastemakers. American Buyers and the Italian Fashion Industry, 1950–55." In. *European Fashion: The Creation of a Global Industry*, edited by R. L. Blaszczyk and V. Pouillard, 146–69. Manchester: Manchester University Press.

Steele, Valerie. 1994. "Italian Fashion and America." In *The Italian Metamorphosis 1943–1968* edited by G. Celant. New York: Guggenheim Museum.

Steele, Valerie. 2003. *Fashion, Italian Style*. New Haven-London: Yale University Press.

Tiratsoo, Nick, and Jim Tomlison. 1997. Exporting the 'Gospel of Productivity': United States Technical Assistance and British Industry, 1945–1960. *Business History Review* 71 (1): 41–81.

Veillon, Dominique. 1990. *La mode sous l'Occupation. Débrouillardise et coquetterie dans la France en guerre (1939–1945)*. Paris: Payot.

Venturelli, Paola. 1997. "Di necessità virtù. La guerra nella moda: da Rosa Genoni al lanital e dintorni." In *Che c'è di nuovo? Niente: la guerra. Donne e uomini nel milanese di fronte alle guerre (1885–1945)*, 419–26. Milan: Mazzotta.

Vergani, Guido. 1992. "La Sala Bianca: Nascita della Moda Italiana." In *La Sala Bianca. Nascita della moda italiana*, edited by G. Malossi, 23–86. Milan: Electa.

White, Nicola. 2000. *Reconstructing Italian Fashion. America and the Development of the Italian Fashion Industry*. Oxford: Berg.

Zamagni, Vera. 1981. *La distribuzione commerciale in Italia fra le due guerre*. Milan: Franco Angeli.

Zanetti, Anna Maria. 1960. "Nasce all'Apem di Vimodrone la nuova moda per tutti." *Cronache della Rinascente-Upim* 13 (19): 5–7.

Zeitlin, Jonathan. 2000. "Introduction." In *Americanization and its Limits. Reworking US Technology and Management in Post-war Europe and Japan*, edited by J. Zeitlin and G. Herrigel, 1–50. New York: Oxford University Press.

CHAPTER 2

Fashion: A Matter of Governance

Abstract Analysing the geography of Italian fashion is a way to assess its fragmentation from an institutional perspective. This chapter examines the various organizations involved in safeguarding and promoting Italian fashion. These actors faced the challenging task of regulating their specific interests to reconcile them with the overall objective of making fashion a stable source of economic growth, while striving to build a genuine fashion system. The analysis sheds light on a variety of contrasting, overlapping, and sometimes even competing governance models that were operating, albeit with varying degrees of effectiveness, from the late 1940s to the mid-1970s. More specifically, in this chapter, we will focus on the organizational structure and main activities of the *Associazione Italiana Industriali dell'Abbigliamento* (AIIA, Italian Clothing Industry Association, 1945), the *Comitato Moda degli Industriali dell'Abbigliamento* (CMIA, Ready-to-Wear Fashion Council, 1959), the *Ente Italiano della Moda* (EIM, Italian Fashion Body, 1951), the *Centro di Firenze per la Moda Italiana* (CFMI, Centre of Florence for Italian Fashion, 1954), and the *Camera Nazionale della Moda Italiana* (CNMI, National Chamber of Italian Fashion, 1962). In the following pages, we will also mention the *Centro Italiano della Moda* of Milan (CIM, Italian Fashion Centre, 1949), the *Comitato della Moda* of Rome (Fashion Committee, 1949), the *Centro Internazionale delle Arti e del Costume* of Venice (CIAC, International Center for the Arts and Costume, 1951), and the *Centro*

E. Merlo and I. Paris, *The Italian Fashion System*, Palgrave Studies in Economic History, https://doi.org/10.1007/978-3-031-52375-5_2

Romano dell'Alta Moda Italiana (CRAMI, Centre of Rome for Italian High Fashion, 1953).

Keywords Italian fashion industry · Fashion institutions · Institutions and economic growth

2.1 The Relational-Centralized Model: The EIM

The *Ente Italiano della Moda* (EIM, Italian Fashion Body) was established in 1951 and represented the continuation of the *Ente Nazionale della Moda* (ENM, National Body of Fashion), founded in 1935. The EIM was headquartered in Turin, a city that, due to its political and industrial centrality, had already been recognized by the fascist government as the Italian capital of fashion. After World War II, even the republican governments started from the premise that the fashion industry was a sector worthy of attention, no longer for reasons of identity, but for political and economic motives. The fashion industry involved multiple stakeholders (both public and private) and had a significant impact on Italy's trade balance. In this context, the fashion industry's objectives would be easier to achieve by organizing the sector according to a centralized governance model, which could promote greater control (including political) and better coordination among all involved.

2.1.1 *The Birth and Rebirth of the EIM*

The EIM rose from the ashes of the ENM, created in 1935 to "Italianize" women's wardrobes and align them with the dictates of fascist autarky. The ENM aimed to institutionalize Italian fashion and sought to control the sector and foster independence from France. The fascist regime considered the regulation of fashion to be part of a broader effort to define a national identity. The establishment of genuinely Italian fashion also had significant economic implications. The ENM's endeavour was ambitious, but it achieved only partial success as, given the influence of French fashion on international markets, both Italian *couturier(e)s* and their clients continued to look to Paris as the reference city.[1]

The EIM was headquartered in Turin, a city that, due to its political and industrial centrality, had already been recognized by the fascist government as the Italian capital of fashion.[2] Even the republican governments of the post-war period started from the premise that the fashion industry was a sector worthy of attention, no longer for reasons of identity, but for political and economic motives. Political and economic institutions are crucial for development and are inextricably linked.[3] The fashion industry involved multiple stakeholders (both public and private) and had a significant impact on Italy's trade balance. In this context, the fashion industry's objectives would be easier to achieve by organizing the sector according to a centralized governance model, which could promote greater control (including political) and better coordination among all involved.

The EIM was officially recognized in 1951 precisely to meet these requirements: to protect the interests of the emerging (and strategic) Italian fashion industry and coordinate initiatives to ensure a more rational use of public funds.[4] The activity of the EIM, however, resumed shortly after the end of World War II. The *Mostra nazionale dell'arte della moda* (National Exhibition of Fashion Art) organized in 1946 at the Royal Palace in Turin was an opportunity to resume the process which had been interrupted by the war. The objective, in this case, was to safeguard a local interest: giving the EIM the role previously held by the ENM and Turin the centrality it had achieved in the first half of the twentieth century. However, the situation of the Italian fashion industry was more complicated and reflected the complexity of the sector. In 1945, the *Associazione Italiana Industriali dell'Abbigliamento* (AIIA, Italian Clothing Industry Association) was founded in Milan. It was a business interest

[1] Gnoli (2000, 17–18, 23–42) and Paulicelli (2004, 76–97). See also Lupano and Vaccari (2009) and Gnoli (2014). On French *haute couture* see De Marly (1980), Lipovetsky (1987), Steele (1999), and Grau (2000).

[2] See Di Castro (1991).

[3] For an overview on this topic see Tylecote (2016), which analyses seminal books that share this view of institutions, and John and Phillips-Fein (2007), which explores the relationships between American business and politics also analysing the role of BIAs. For an overview of the Italian case, see Di Martino and Vasta (2017, 183–230).

[4] L'Abbigliamento Italiano (AI) (1960a).

association which aimed to provide a reference point for the ready-to-wear companies. A few years later (1949), two other entities were born in Milan (CIM, *Centro Italiano della Moda*) and in Rome (*Comitato della Moda*), which aspired to take on the legacy of the ENM and lead the entire sector.[5]

In this dynamic context, which included the city of Venice with its *Centro Internazionale delle Arti e del Costume* (CIAC, International Centre of Arts and Costume, 1951), the previously mentioned Giovanni Battista Giorgini would also be involved. In 1951, he organized the first Italian Fashion Show in Florence. The similar timing of the start of the Florentine fashion shows and the government's recognition of the EIM might be merely coincidental. However, the choice to exclude the high fashion houses of Turin from the Italian Fashion Show was far from accidental. The partial reconciliation between Florence and Turin that occurred in the months following was definitively compromised in 1954. The *Centro di Firenze per la Moda Italiana* (CFMI, Centre of Florence for Italian Fashion)—whose purpose was to manage the fashion shows at *Palazzo Pitti*—was founded, shortly after the establishment of the SIAM (*Sindacato Italiano di Alta Moda*, Italian High Fashion Union, 1953) in Rome, which later became the *Centro Romano dell'Alta Moda Italiana* (CRAMI, Centre of Rome for Italian High Fashion). The emerging picture was, therefore, extremely fragmented, as SIAM's statute expressly prohibited Roman fashion houses from participating in the Italian Fashion Show.[6] If Turin and Florence were distant, the gap between Florence and Rome was also widening.

In the early 1950s, the Italian fashion industry was in full swing, and the situation that had arisen indicated a process of decentralization rather than coordination and collaboration. The rivalry between Florence, Rome, Milan, and Turin had given rise to numerous institutional entities, each playing a role in the governance, protection, and promotion of national fashion. These actors had a role in the construction of Italian fashion that was autonomous from a technical and artistic point of view. However, in many other aspects (starting from organizational and promotional questions), overlaps, conflicts, and inefficiencies were created. The risk of compromising the development of the sector was high, and for this

[5] Paris (2006, 187–90), Capalbo (2012, 142).

[6] Capalbo (2012, 144–46).

reason, the EIM was officially identified as the reference body. The EIM was not intended to replace the other entities but to perform a coordinating role, involving all stakeholders in the sector, from promotion to rationalization of the calendar of major events, with a particular emphasis on fostering synergies between the worlds of creation and industry.[7]

The project which aimed to (re)centralize the EIM, while keeping it under political control, was born under the worst of auspices. The establishment of the *Camera Nazionale della Moda Italiana* (CNMI, National Chamber of Italian fashion) in 1962 confirmed that tensions were far from being resolved. No one was willing to relinquish their role and leave matters in the hands of others. The CNMI, supported by CFMI and CRAMI and later extended to Milanese fashion houses, aimed to coordinate the various actors of Italian fashion. However, it was heavily biased towards high fashion. The latter still occupied the top of the production chain, and precisely because of this leadership role, the CNMI aspired to lead the entire Italian fashion sector. It represented the reference point for the main Italian *couturier(e)s*, and they considered it the only entity that could legitimately protect their interests. Just as the AIIA served as a unique interlocutor for the ready-to-wear industry, the CNMI provided the high fashion sector with a single representative. This was undoubtedly an important achievement, despite the sometimes strained relations between the Roman and Florentine members. However, the objective of claiming leadership of the sector was not forgotten, leading to fierce competition between the CNMI and the EIM throughout the 1960s and 1970s.

2.1.2 Organizational Structure and Activities

One of the factors influencing an association's ability to pursue its own strategies is the quality of its internal organization.[8] Business history studies still underestimate the importance of the activities carried out and services offered by these organizations in achieving their statutory objectives, as well as enhancing their attractiveness.[9]

[7] Simonetto (1953).

[8] Coleman and Jacek (1983, 278–80), Doner and Schneider (2000, 270–75).

[9] Ville (2007, 301–3).

To better understand the role played not only by the EIM but, more generally, by all the subjects analysed in this chapter, it is therefore necessary to examine these two aspects as well. The lack of archive material is largely compensated by the in-depth reports on the EIM's activities periodically published in the specialized magazine *L'Abbigliamento Italiano*, the official organ of the EIM.

If the CNMI appeared too biased towards high fashion to be considered an impartial guide, the EIM might have seemed too focused on the needs of industry, which over the years had consolidated and then concentrated along the Turin-Milan axis (and more generally in Piedmont and Lombardy). It was not accidental that almost all members were illustrious representatives of the ready-to-wear industry, most of whom were based in these two geographical areas.[10] The needs of large-scale industrial production drove the more modern enterprises to locations where the conditions for development were present. Turin and Milan offered infrastructure, services, financial capital, and skilled and unskilled workforce, as well as proximity to the most important Italian and European markets.

The EIM had legal status, was apolitical, and had non-profit objectives. Unlike the CNMI and the AIIA, it did not carry out trade union activities. All individuals, companies, and organizations directly involved in fashion were eligible for membership. However, it had strong ties with the political world and the city of Turin. The founding decree law of February 1951 identified the EIM as the sole entity with specific competence in the field of clothing and fashion. The General Council, responsible for managing the EIM, was appointed by decree law of the Ministry of Industry and Commerce and included members chosen by the Chamber of Commerce and the Municipality of Turin. The President was also proposed by the same Minister and appointed by the Prime Minister.[11]

While the textile and ready-to-wear industries were closely observing the EIM, the same cannot be said for *couturier(e)s*. This partially explains why the EIM remained effectively inactive until at least the early 1960s. In fact, there were pressures exerted by the CNMI itself to delay the process

[10] E.g., see L'Abbigliamento Italiano (AI) (1960e).

[11] AI (1959c, 1960c); see also Ente Italiano della Moda (1966a).

of institutional recognition, accusing the EIM of being completely disconnected from the interests of high fashion.[12] The political class, while not accepting its demands, did not fail to support the establishment of the CNMI, thus legitimizing it politically.[13] In the early 1960s, therefore, the EIM resumed its activities in a context of profound uncertainty. However, it remained the awareness of the need for greater coordination between different activities and closer collaboration among all parties involved in Italian fashion, from ready-to-wear to high fashion, from textile industries, footwear, and accessories to distribution, from the specialized press to governmental bodies.[14]

The statutory objective of the EIM was to coordinate, strengthen, and enhance the creative and productive activities of the fashion industry, directing its work and assisting the various parties also in the promotional phase (with special attention paid to foreign markets). Therefore, the EIM recognized collaboration as one of the main issues to address in order to support the growth of the sector. Such an approach was even more necessary in a highly fragmented context such as that of the early 1960s: in terms of production, with the industry still divided into two relatively disconnected realities (high fashion and ready-to-wear); from a commercial and promotional perspective, with a proliferation of events often of dubious quality and usefulness; and from an institutional point of view, due to the presence of numerous associations and organizations, each vying to represent part or all of the Italian fashion industry.

Overall, the Italian fashion industry was in need of regulation, although the stimuli that should have favoured this process were still weak. From the perspective of its relations with other fashion institutions, in particular, the EIM faced competition from the CNMI, which did not hesitate to overstep its prerogatives and thus detract from its usefulness. Along with the difficulties encountered in finding the necessary financial resources to operate and the strained relations with more qualified press (which paid only scant attention to the activities of the EIM, preferring other organizations such as the CNMI), these are some of the reasons that best explain its slow decline. However, the EIM's inability to renew itself emerges as

[12] AI (1962a).

[13] See the letters addressed to the CNMI in Archivio Storico della Camera Nazionale della Moda Italiana (ASCNMI), b. 4.

[14] AI (1959b, 1960a, 1960h, 1960i).

a key factor, gradually proving itself less suited to govern the new course the fashion industry was taking. First and foremost, there was difficulty in dealing with the radical changes that occurred during the 1960s, resulting in the incapacity to manage the 'fashion variable' and especially to coordinate the entire production chain, from creation to distribution. The statutory reform envisaged in the early 1970s, which aimed to reaffirm the EIM's responsibility to protect the general interests of the sector rather than just those of certain categories, effectively confirmed the limited results achieved until that time in terms of coordination. Therefore, the EIM had fallen short of its main statutory objective, partly due to the profound changes that had changed traditional production and organizational models.[15] The EIM promoted thorough and constant research activity, which, starting from the second half of the 1960s, focused on the structure of demand in the female market, the younger generations, and the impact of fashion on the structure of production. This work confirmed that the EIM was on the right track, but it failed to translate this significant knowledge and interpretative effort into concrete actions.

The EIM mostly suffered from the lack of involvement of all the actors of the Italian fashion industry (from high fashion to the specialized press) and, above all, the not always collaborative attitude of the various institutions involved. In this regard, the opinion of the renowned French *couturier* Balmain is significant. He praised the quality of Italian fashion but emphasized the absence of a shared vision, limiting the ability to provide a clear direction to the entire sector.[16] What was lacking, therefore, was not bureaucratic coordinating bodies, but the willingness of individual actors to collaborate with each other. The difficulties encountered by the EIM ultimately stemmed from a highly centralized and authoritarian management, which came under the control of Amos Ciabattoni, who until then had been the Secretary-General of the CNMI.[17] The organization of the *Conferenza della Moda* (Fashion Meeting) in May 1975 was supposed to be an opportunity to analyse and finally address the real issues facing the Italian fashion system. However,

[15] AI (1970, 1971b, 1971c, 1972).

[16] AI (1959a) and Linea (1961).

[17] Ciabattoni was one of the most authoritative figures in Italian fashion and a key figure in understanding the institutional dynamics of this industry. Ciabattoni held top positions in organizations such as CRAMI and the CNMI, and also served as a board member for major textile companies such as Lanerossi.

despite clearly framing the fundamental questions, it did not lead to any concrete action and effectively marked the end of the EIM—which was finally abolished in 1977.[18]

While EIM failed in terms of building a new Italian fashion system, it did not fail to make an important contribution to the international affirmation of the Italian fashion through well-organized promotion activities. Overall, the results achieved in this field were positive. The organization of promotional and commercial events in Italy and abroad was one of the most commonly used tools. Numerous reports on this matter can be found in the pages of *L'Abbigliamento Italiano*.[19] Among these, the first initiative organized in the spring of 1960 stands out, firstly because it marked the beginning of the EIM's activity in this field, but above all because the event organized in South Africa allows us to highlight many elements common to all these initiatives.[20] Firstly, the destination, which signalled the attention given to foreign markets, particularly focusing on emerging markets. Although apparently debatable and criticized by some observers, the choice of South Africa had, in fact, been carefully studied, considering the characteristics and potential of the market, both in terms of size and purchasing power, as well as the tastes and needs of the local consumers.

These initiatives aimed to support Italian clothing in all its forms. In the case of the South African event, which involved meetings at the most important department stores, prestigious high fashion houses (such as Schuberth of Rome and Enzo of Milan) were present, as well as significant ready-to-wear and fur companies (such as Apem, Ballarini, Krizia, and Ruggeri). However, the occasion also served to promote the textile and accessories industry, as each garment was made with Italian fabrics and accompanied by Italian-made footwear, hats, bags, gloves, stockings, jewellery, etc. Rather than being just a spectacular display, these events had a purely commercial purpose, and the choice of prestigious department stores as event locations further demonstrated this. The aim was to support the entire Italian fashion supply chain, with particular attention to industrial production. However, the desire to promote a total look which was entirely Italian marked a higher goal: to promote, through fashion, a

[18] Textilia (1975) and Bottero (1979, 281–83).

[19] E.g., Rossetti (1963) and Robiola (1967, 1968).

[20] AI (1960b, 1960d, 1960f) and Ricciotti (1960).

broader concept of 'Made in Italy' and all the products associated with it. Besides facilitating short-to-medium-term trade agreements, the ultimate goal was to create a positive sentiment towards Italy and all products of Italian origin.

While it might be complex to assess the impact of these initiatives on the international consolidation of the Made in Italy brand, it is more straightforward to measure their commercial return. Reports confirm that the success of these events often coincided with an increase in demand not only for clothing but also for other related products such as accessories and footwear, or even products from other sectors like crystalware and various decorative items. Concerning clothing, the ready-to-wear sector benefited the most. The presence of high fashion houses diminished within a few years, with missions increasingly focused on so-called industrial fashion (ranging from clothing to accessories). It is not unlikely that the difficult relationship with the CNMI might have had an influence. However, the success achieved in terms of public visibility and sales suggests that the presence of high fashion as a marketing lever was no longer indispensable. This is because Italian ready-to-wear had gradually enhanced its appeal even in foreign markets, a result confirmed by the growing success of one of the most important specialized markets in the sector—SAMIA (*Salone Mercato Internazionale dell'Abbigliamento*, International Clothing Market) in Turin. For instance, the exhibition *Italien in Hamburg* in 1962 selected only manufacturers of textiles, clothing, knitwear, footwear, leather goods, and accessories.[21] The presentation of Italian products in the shop windows of the city, the screening of documentaries, and the organization of conferences and concerts complemented the initiative and, following proven formulas, contributed as much to the success of Italian fashion as to the promotion of a Made in Italy brand that could now evoke more than the material aspects of production.

The promotional activity of the EIM was of great importance to Italian businesses as it allowed them to exploit the potential offered by the process of closer European economic integration. The goal was to gain greater prestige in the international market to partially compensate for the small scale and rigidity of the domestic market. Collaboration with the *Istituto per il Commercio Estero* (ICE, Italian Trade Agency) was crucial.

[21] AI (1962b).

The ICE assisted the EIM in the selection and organization of many of the events held abroad. The fashion sector was considered a strategic area within the framework of the Italian economy and, therefore, deserved the full collaboration of a public institution designed specifically to develop, facilitate, and promote Italy's economic and commercial relations with foreign countries (with particular attention to the needs of small and medium-sized enterprises).[22] The ICE played a central role in the promotional strategy of Italian fashion, especially for the industrial product. The ready-to-wear companies (and this also applied to high fashion houses participating in the initiatives) did not have the financial and organizational resources necessary to independently manage missions abroad. The ICE not only allowed the coverage of substantial expenses, but thanks to its offices located around the world, it was able to prepare events taking into account the structure of target markets and the needs of the local clientele. At the same time, it could also negotiate commercial and promotional agreements. These initiatives provided visibility to the entire textile and clothing supply chain, promoting both well-established brands and smaller, lesser-known enterprises alike.

2.1.3 Fashion Fairs: SAMIA and MITAM

Among the activities of the EIM, it is worth noting its participation in the organization of a significant market specialized in 'industrial fashion' such as the aforementioned SAMIA in Turin, one of the major international promotional and commercial events for ready-to-wear. Since its first edition in November 1955, SAMIA also served as a testing ground for some of the significant early collaborations between ready-to-wear companies and high fashion designers. In this case, the stimulus for collaboration came from industry rather than high fashion, but the objective was always to target an intermediate market segment.[23] Overall, SAMIA was a successful experiment, and until the end of the 1960s, it made Turin the capital of Italian ready-to-wear.[24]

[22] See Nocentini (2005a, 2005b, 2007).

[23] Paris (2010b, 135–39).

[24] Ente Italiano della Moda (1966b).

SAMIA was also a novelty from an organizational perspective. While high fashion subordinated every promotional strategy to strict regulations (especially after the establishment of the CNMI), the ready-to-wear industry was much more flexible. The increasingly demanding market called for new promotional and commercial structures that facilitated dialogue among the various stakeholders in Italian fashion (including the press), and SAMIA moved in this direction. Exhibitions, fairs, and fashion weeks were not new in Europe, but the distinction between a trade fair and a specialized market was significant. Within a period of seven days and in a single location, Turin offered a comprehensive overview ranging from clothing and knitwear to footwear and accessories. The organizational structure was highly agile and efficient. Therefore, SAMIA set an example not only for traditionally advanced countries like France, but also for different market sectors such as textiles. Among the specialized European markets that emerged following the organizational model of SAMIA were the *Salon du Prêt-à-porter*, *Interstoff*, *Marché Textile International*, and in Italy, MITAM (*Mercato Internazionale del Tessile per l'Abbigliamento e l'Arredamento*, International Textile Market for Clothing and Furnishing) in Milan.

The structure of SAMIA fully met commercial requirements rather than promotional objectives. The focus, indeed, was not on the fashion shows (although they were present and partially open to the public and specialized press), but on the dozens of stands where thousands of buyers could freely view and handle the merchandise before striking deals. The daily fashion shows served only to condense the extensive range of production on display, keeping the spotlight on individual companies (presenting two to four garments per stand). The objective was to save time for buyers, quickly directing them to the companies most suitable to meet their needs. This approach was substantially different from the Italian Fashion Show in Florence, where the fashion shows were at least as important as the days dedicated to negotiations, due to the media coverage they attracted.

With this particular format, SAMIA aimed to achieve specific objectives. Firstly, to establish direct contacts between ready-to-wear producers, buyers, and distributors from around the world. This approach allowed for cost and time savings. Secondly, SAMIA sought to provide space for both well-known and new companies. The organizers were well aware of buyers' interest in novelty, marking yet another difference from the high fashion catwalks of Florence. Numerous services were designed to ensure the efficient presentation of collections and to facilitate contact with buyers, as well as to attract journalists, technicians, and everyone interested in the Italian fashion industry. Finally, SAMIA organized appointments for the entire industrial production, from clothing to accessories. It involved not only stands and fashion shows, but also various meetings and events, which made SAMIA a useful tool to promote a coordinated and curated image of the entire production chain.

The numbers confirm the success of SAMIA, which, by the middle of the decade, was considered one of the three most important European events for industrially produced clothing (alongside IGEDO in Düsseldorf and the *Salon du Prêt-à-porter* in Paris). The majority of foreign buyers came from Europe (particularly from Germany, Switzerland, France, and the UK), further distinguishing it from the Italian Fashion Show of Florence, where most foreign buyers came from the United States. The experience of SAMIA thus confirmed Italy's ability to develop original promotional strategies through the actions of individual fashion institutions, adapting to the peculiarities of the production structure and the characteristics of its target market. Moreover, as in Florence, Turin also aimed to develop high-quality ready-to-wear, following in the footsteps of the French *prêt-à-porter*. While in Florence, the initiative originated from high fashion designers using the name *alta moda pronta* (high fashion ready-to-wear), in Torino, it was the ready-to-wear industries that supported the project. In 1969, an ad hoc event called *Modaselezione* was launched in an attempt to develop and launch higher-quality clothing (the so-called *confezione di lusso*, luxury ready-to-wear), catering for an intermediate market segment. From an institutional perspective, it was competing with the Florentine event.[25] At the first edition, scheduled one week after the end of the Florentine fashion shows, and therefore giving rise to new disagreements with high fashion houses and reference institutions,[26] more than 160 exhibitors participated (including well-known names such as Cori-Biki, Sidi, Genny Creazioni, Miss Rosier, Pirelliconfezioni, and Sportmax), along with over 270 international buyers.[27]

[25] Robiola (1969) and Marroncini (1972).

[26] E.g., see ASCNMI, b. 221, f. 221-2, *Disposizioni della Camera per una eventuale partecipazione delle case a "Moda Selezione"*; ASCNMI, b. 230, f. 230-2, *Manifestazione Firenze - Moda Selezione*.

[27] AI (1969a, 1969b, 1969c, 1969d).

The gradual opening of Florence to companies that had previously found their ideal location in Turin, however, diminished interest in this initiative and marked the beginning of the decline of Turin as the centre of industrial clothing production. The 1960s represented a turning point for these aspects as well. The changing structure of demand rendered these events increasingly anachronistic, leading to a radical transformation or, as in the case of SAMIA, rapid decline.

The events sponsored by the EIM included MITAM, a specialized textile market that was first held in 1957 at the *Fiera Campionaria* in Milan (Milan Sample Fair). This initiative confirmed the strength of the Turin-Milan axis regarding industrial production and the EIM's commitment, in line with its main statutory objective, to involve more members of the supply chain. Like SAMIA, MITAM had a strong commercial character. Nevertheless, there was also a desire to make it a place of collaboration between the textile industry and the ready-to-wear sector.[28]

However, MITAM also reflected the existing institutional conflict. The idea belonged to the CIM in Milan, which had resorted to organizing a specialized market for textiles only after missing the opportunity to set up similar for the ready-to-wear sector. The opposition from the EIM, which was engaged in the establishment of SAMIA, halted the Milanese initiative, which had already approached the Ministry of Industry for the necessary authorizations. The reason was simple: approving the CIM project would have officially declared the EIM to be useless, as it was the only legally recognized entity in the field of fashion at the time.[29] The birth of MITAM, therefore, was meant to rebalance and, at the same time, strengthen relations with Turin. A close connection between MITAM, the EIM, and SAMIA remained. The secretariat of MITAM was initially entrusted to Vladimiro Rossini (General Director of the EIM), and the presidency to Dino Alfieri (President of CIM in Milan). The management bodies also included Dario Morelli (President of the EIM and SAMIA) and Giulio Goehring (President of the AIIA, based in Milan).[30]

The results achieved by MITAM were satisfactory and helped the Italian textile sector overcome the severe economic downturn that had hit

[28] See Paris (2006, 293–301).

[29] Linea (1955) and Bottero (1979, 51–52).

[30] Misia (1957) and AI (1966).

the cotton and wool sectors hard in the early 1960s.[31] Although in its first 25 editions MITAM attracted almost 100,000 buyers (half of whom came from around a hundred foreign countries),[32] it was gradually replaced and permanently closed in 1975.

The EIM inevitably followed the fate of SAMIA and MITAM. The closure of the CRAMI and the downsizing of the Florentine fashion shows in *Palazzo Pitti* confirmed, however, that the issues concerned not only the industrial sector. Starting from the mid-1970s, the old models of production and consumption, outdated commercial and promotional strategies, and anachronistic governance structures of the Italian fashion industry made way for new realities that completed the process of formation of the Italian fashion system.

2.2 The Municipal Model: The CFMI

The fashion shows organized in Florence by Giovanni Giorgini soon transformed from events intended for a small circle of friends and acquaintances into a fixed appointment of international importance. With the increasing number of participants, the Italian Fashion Show became a complex event from an organizational perspective and was financially burdensome. However, the organization of the initial editions continued to be delegated to private initiative and, in particular, relied on Giorgini's network of contacts. The establishment of the CFMI in 1954 represented the institutional response to the changes brought about by the individual initiative of the Florentine buyer. Its articulated evolutionary path can be divided into three periods: that between its foundation and Giorgini's departure (1967); a time of severe crisis that continued until the mid-1980s; and finally, the period that began with the process of relaunching Florence, which over time consolidated the Tuscan capital as an international trade fair centre for companies producing men's fashion, casual and sportswear.

[31] ASCNMI, b. 3, *Relazione del Consiglio direttivo all'Assemblea generale dei soci del 16 Dicembre 1967*, pp. 34–36.

[32] Giras (1969).

2.2.1 *Florence and the CFMI: The New Capital of Italian Fashion?*

In 1954, the municipal administration, the Chamber of Commerce, and the Florence Tourism Board provided Giovanni Giorgini with the financial resources to establish the CFMI. This initiative aimed to fill an evident institutional gap. While Florence had become an attraction for international commercial operators and media, it had not yet become home to an operational institution representing Italian fashion. Once again, the objective was to represent Italian fashion both nationally and internationally, following the example of those institutions in other Italian cities that pursued similar goals. In Turin, as we have seen, the EIM was established, while in Milan, the CIM had been operational since 1949. Also in this case the objective was the coordination of all Italian fashion activities, the separation of which was considered to be the greatest obstacle to the expansion of the industry in Italy and beyond. The city of Milan, which boasted well-established relationships with foreign markets, was thought to provide the best context to facilitate the achievement of the organization's goals. Despite being located in Milan, the CIM organized promotional activities also in other foreign and Italian cities such as the Fashion Festival in Venice, where the *Centro Internazionale delle Arti e del Costume* (CIAC) had been founded in 1951. In Rome, the first Fashion National Congress that the local Chamber of Commerce had organized in 1949 paved the way for the establishment of the *Comitato della Moda* (Roman Fashion Committee). The new association was aimed at strengthening and increasing the fashion-related production activities which benefitted from Rome being the Italian political capital, and at maintaining constant and active relationships with all national and foreign fashion centres for the technical, artistic, and professional development of Italian production.

The establishment of the CFMI was the result of a process which built upon a project conceived by Giorgini in 1952.[33] The project identified the main centres for the promotion of Italian high fashion in the cities of Florence and Rome, with Giorgini himself as the organizer and coordinator of these activities. The plan envisaged maintaining the headquarters

[33] The history of the CFMI summarized here has been meticulously reconstructed by Pinchera (2009, 60–79) based on documents preserved in the Archivio della Moda Italiana of Giovanni Battista Giorgini and in the Historical Archive of the Chamber of Commerce of Florence.

of the EIM in Turin in exchange for the cessation of the activities of the CIM in Milan. The EIM itself would undergo a transformation, becoming a representative entity not only of the tailoring industry but also, or even primarily, of industrial production. Three giants of Italian industrial production—Italviscosa, Cotonificio Valle di Susa, and Lanifici Rivetti, which produced artificial fibres, cotton, and wool respectively—would be given positions within the management bodies of the EIM. In Giorgini's plan, the honorary presidency of the EIM would be assigned to another important figure in the national textile industry, Franco Marinotti, the President of Snia Viscosa.

The agreement was reached and ratified in November 1952. Giorgini and Oreste Rivetti were appointed as the new vice presidents of the EIM, which would sponsor the Florentine events under the new name "Giorgini's High Fashion Showings". The promotional activities would be placed under the aegis of a Promotional Committee headed by the operational president of the EIM (Count Filippo Giordano delle Lanze) and the Mayor of Florence. The organizational and managerial responsibilities were assigned to an autonomous Executive Committee with full powers, chaired by Giorgini himself. In addition to this, Maria Ciulli Ruggeri (representing the Government), Stefano Rivetti (grandson of the founder of Lanifici Rivetti), Olga De Grésy (founder of the knitwear company Mirsa, present in Florence since the very first fashion shows), and finally, Emilio Discacciati (Cotonificio Valle di Susa) and Dino Alfieri (Snia Viscosa) were appointed as EIM delegates.

However, contrary to the initial plan, the CIM in Milan was not closed. Its founder, the aforementioned President of Snia Viscosa, Franco Marinotti, managed to firmly link its fortunes with the most technologically advanced part of the Italian textile industry.[34] In this context, Marinotti's role is central to understanding the institutional dynamics of the sector. Marinotti was also the founder of the previously mentioned *Centro Internazionale delle Arti e del Costume* of Venice (CIAC, International Center for the Arts and Costume, 1951). As specified in its statute, the CIAC aimed to organize artistic and cultural events in the field of arts and costume.[35] The composition of the first Executive Committee

[34] Colli (2003), Spadoni (2006), and Bertilorenzi, Cerretano, and Perugini (2022).

[35] ASCNMI, b. 16, f. 16-7, *Statuto del Centro internazionale delle arti e del costume* (art. 1).

(article 3 of the statute) left no doubts about the direction it intended to take, making it unique among the associations that crowded the world of Italian fashion. Some members of the Executive Committee (Furio Cicogna, Alighiero De Micheli, and Giovanni Balella) and the Secretary-General (Paolo Marinotti, son of Franco)[36] were united by a shared in-depth knowledge of the textile industry and artificial fibres. De Micheli, Cicogna, and Marinotti had, in fact, held entrepreneurial and managerial roles in the sector. Likewise, Balella was not unfamiliar with this world, as in an autarchic context, at the end of the 1930s, he had been tasked by the Fascist government to maintain contacts with companies (including Snia Viscosa itself) that could potentially utilize cellulose obtained from Italian agricultural products and plants from African colonies.[37]

The purposes for which the CIAC was established, as well as the composition of its initial Board of Directors, reveal that the founders had very clear ideas on the link between art and industry. This relationship was not meant to be confined to patronage and collecting, but rather to focus on the search for new, highly technological materials to be used in the production of aesthetically pleasing goods. The combination of fashion with artificial and synthetic fibres was one of the most important testing grounds. Fashion had long been in constant dialogue with avant-garde art and was gradually establishing itself as a sector with promising industrial prospects. Artificial and synthetic fibres represented the cutting edge of scientific and technological research applied to the industry. They were the quintessential symbol of contemporary modernity and could give new impetus to the already mature textile and ready-to-wear industry. Therefore, it is not surprising that the CIAC also organized fashion exhibitions with specific themes, aimed at encouraging fashion designers to use textile fibres produced by Snia Viscosa.[38] From an institutional perspective, the connection between art and industry was expressed through the alignment of intentions between the CIAC in Venice and the CIM in Milan, which was guaranteed by the presence of Franco and Paolo Marinotti in their respective governing bodies. While the CIAC occupied a different position compared to CFMI, the same cannot be said for the CIM. Contrary to what Giorgini had envisaged, the CIM continued to operate,

[36] Collicelli Cagol (2008).

[37] Petri (2006), Ferretti (2011), and Cerretano (2020).

[38] Paris (2006, 188).

thereby bringing into question both the EIM's ability to represent the entire industrial supply chain and Florence's ambition to establish itself as the new capital of Italian fashion.

2.2.2 Organizational Structure and Activities

The agreement ratified at the end of 1952 represented an important milestone for Giorgini and for the city of Florence, but not necessarily for the entire Italian fashion industry. In essence, evident differences persisted not only between Rome and Florence but also between Turin and Milan. The question of the link with industry also remained. The objective of involving the textile industry had been achieved, and the active support of its most representative figures was also obtained. However, with the exception of Dino Alfieri from Snia on the CFMI's Executive Committee as the EIM delegate, the CFMI had lost the backing of the man-made fibre industry—that is, the part of the production chain that represented the future of the textile industry itself and revolved around the CIM in Milan and the CIAC in Venice.

The position of Giorgini and Florence within the national context had, however, been strengthened. Giorgini's role as the official organizer and coordinator of high fashion events was officially recognized. Consequently, he could initiate institutional and financial collaborations that would soon establish Florence as the base for a new operational entity for the Italian fashion industry. Giorgini's winning strategies had been twofold: forming an alliance with certain representatives of the textile industry and securing the assured support of the Florentine city authorities, who had committed to funding the fashion shows.

The new organization, established under the Statute of 1954, was named the CFMI and was based in *Palazzo Strozzi*. It was a non-profit association with both public and private participation. Local institutions held prominent positions from the outset. Alongside the EIM, the sponsors of the centre included all city bodies: the Municipality, the Provincial Tourism Board, the Autonomous Tourism Agency, the Chamber of Commerce, Industry, Agriculture, and the Association of Industrialists. The primary objective was to promote and develop any initiatives aimed at enhancing Italian fashion in all its aspects. Events and presentations intended for international buyers were considered of paramount importance. The administration and management were entrusted to the Executive Committee, comprising representatives from various supporting entities and external members such as Giorgini, who was officially appointed as the organizer of the Florentine initiatives. The Executive Committee prepared the budgets and balance sheets for the various editions of the events and managed the use of various financial contributions. Starting from 1955, the Florentine fashion shows began to be directly sponsored by the CFMI and were no longer, as in the first four editions, under the direct patronage of Giorgini or, as in 1953 and 1954, under the aegis of the EIM (which had, in the meantime, been placed under administration following the resignation of President Furio Cicogna).[39]

After the establishment of the CFMI, the number of buyers and journalists attending the Florentine fashion shows increased significantly. The number of fashion houses participating and number of garments presented also grew. During the second half of the 1950s, the number of buyers and press at the *Pitti* Fashion Shows increased—reaching 600 people from 13 countries in 1959, although this figure mainly comprised German and US buyers. Between the end of the 1950s and the beginning of the 1960s, the number of fashion houses present, as well as the models presented, also increased.[40]

Giorgini stepped down from the presidency of the CFMI in 1967, marking the beginning of a new phase in the history of the organization. His decision was probably influenced by difficult relations with local institutions and other associations in the sector, along with the realization that the Florentine venture had reached maturity. He was succeeded by Franco Tancredi, who had previously served as a councillor for the CFMI, President of the Provincial Tourism Board of Florence, and a member of the organizing committee for Italian high fashion events. Tancredi held the position until 1987, and the two decades of his presidency coincided with a period of increasing autonomy for the CFMI from national fashion institutions. The Florentine events transformed into a trade fair, characterized

[39] Decree of the Prime Minister 1 June 1 1954, *Gazzetta Ufficiale della Repubblica Italiana*, 95, n. 137, 18 June 1954: 1894; Decree of the Prime Minister 23 June 1955, *Gazzetta Ufficiale della Repubblica Italiana*, 96, n. 158, 12 July 1955: 2519.

[40] Pinchera and Rinallo (2020, 11). Further data concerning the number of buyers attending the Florentine fashion shows between 1964 and 1973 show a declining trend until 1967, followed by a huge increase that brought the number to almost 3700 (Paris, 2010b).

by a growing degree of specialization and openness to the participation of industrial enterprises.[41]

In 1968, the CFMI organized the first edition of MAIT (*Mostra Campionaria della Maglieria*, Knitwear Sample Fair), a specialized trade show for high fashion knitwear. In 1969, the first men's ready-to-wear fashion show was held, in addition to the boutique fashion and knitwear shows. 1972 saw the first edition of *Pitti Uomo*, a trade fair for men's clothing and accessories, which quickly became one of the most important international fashion trade events for men's fashion. Following the success of *Pitti Uomo*, the CFMI organized new fairs such as *Pitti Bimbo* in 1975, *Pitti Filati* in 1977, and *Pitti Casa* in 1978, reflecting the process of market segmentation in the fashion industry that was rapidly accelerating at the time.[42]

However, the diversification of fashion events could not prevent the crisis of Florence as a trade fair hub, evident since the early 1970s. In 1971, one month before the start of the spring knitwear and boutique fashion shows, the American magazine *Women's Wear Daily* published a series of rather unsettling news articles, relayed by the ANSA News Agency: Walter Albini and the five ready-to-wear companies with which the young designer held a collaboration contract would showcase their collections in Milan rather than Florence. Two other important brands, Krizia and Missoni, had decided to honour their commitments, but they cancelled their subsequent presentations in the autumn. The opinion of Luciano Papini of Misterfox, one of the companies for which Albini provided stylistic consultation, reflected the unfolding situation when he stated that buyers were now only coming to Florence to make appointments for Milan.[43] Florence had become synonymous with rigidity, burdened by a series of constraints that restricted both the creative and commercial phases. In contrast, far from *Palazzo Pitti*, one could more carefully select the buyers, present more extensive collections (in Florence, only 20 clothing items could be showcased), and, above all, freely choose the setting and scenography of the presentation to better enhance the collection. The formality of the shows was less suited to a

[41] Bottero (1979, 164–66), ASCNMI, box 16, f. 16-6, Press release, 2 August 1968.

[42] Lavanga (2018) and Turra (2021).

[43] ASCNMI, b. 16, f. 16-6, *Notiziario moda ANSA*, 18 March 1971.

type of production aimed at a young and dynamic market segment.[44] Given this challenge to the status of the Florence catwalk, many *griffe* moved the presentation of their collections to Milan.[45]

The crisis in Florence reached its peak in the mid-1980s. In 1984, the last *Pitti Donna* event was held (the 68th edition), it was already facing significant difficulties due to competition from fashion shows in Milan. Despite its innovative aspects, the CFMI's strategy had remained rooted in tradition, which understood fashion as an expression of a local production milieu. Attempts to counter Milan's rise by claiming exclusive Florentine ownership of the birth of Italian fashion and the invention of *alta moda pronta*, or by relying on the agreement reached with Rome for the joint management of the fashion show calendar, were all signs of weakness.[46] Such arguments were ineffective against the potential expressed by the new capital of fashion (Milan), which, among other advantages, had the benefit of not having to deal with any burdensome past history.

The period in the history of the CFMI, from its foundation in 1954 to Giorgini's withdrawal in 1967, is of particular interest to better understand the process of formation of the Italian fashion system. Giorgini's project aimed to create a centre dedicated to the management of fashion shows, which were considered a fundamental promotional asset for the international reputation and economic success of Italian fashion. In this context, the role of Florence as the capital of Italian fashion would have been strengthened further. As evidenced by the relationships built with representatives from the industry, Giorgini's project went beyond these objectives, identifying in Florence and the Florentine fashion shows the foundation of a fashion system created through the involvement of institutions as well as the entire production chain.

[44] ASCNMI, b. 185, f. 185-1, *Norme e regolamento per la partecipazione delle case*; b. 185, f. 185-4, *Rapporto ANIBO*.

[45] See, for example, the case of Mila Schön in ASCNMI, b. 176, f. 176-9, *Prezzi minimi e massimi e relative polemiche* (letter of 24 October 1967 from Mila Schön to Paolo Faina, president of the CNMI, and letter of 7 November 1967 from Mila Schön to Amos Ciabattoni, General Secretary of the CNMI).

[46] The president of CFMI, Franco Tancredi, also served as a member of the organizing committee for events in Italian high fashion, whose main task was precisely to coordinate the fashion shows in Rome and Florence.

The financial dependence on local entities soon revealed the difficulty in reconciling the origins, nature, and municipal roots of the CFMI with the endeavour to establish itself as a cornerstone of the Italian fashion system. As Pinchera asserts, the fate of *Pitti* relied largely on income derived from the buyers themselves and the funding from public city entities, which, in the early 1960s, covered the vast majority of the costs of Florentine activities (50–60% and 30%, respectively). The Ministry of Foreign Trade also contributed to CFMI's funding, yet the amount during the same period did not exceed 10% of the needs (approximately 6 million lire). Contrary to assurances and despite being in precarious financial conditions, no contribution was received from the EIM. Meanwhile, the textile industry supplied approximately half of the promised 16 million lire. Ultimately, the international success of the events (which attracted an increasing number of buyers) and Giorgini's personal relationships with some of the key figures of the city's institutions (particularly with Giacomo Devoto, President of the Chamber of Commerce, and with Mario Vannini Parenti and Franco Tancredi, two presidents of the local Tourist Board) saved the fate of both Giorgini and the Florentine events.[47] The importance of Giovanni Giorgini to the Florentine project was evident, but at the same time, this represented both a strength and a fragility of the entire project.

It is not surprising, therefore, that despite some ups and downs, for Giorgini and the CFMI, it was a much more realistic goal to aim for a strategic position in the international fashion landscape through fashion shows than to create an Italian fashion system. During the 1950s and 1960s, the Florentine shows followed the evolution of market demands and emerging opportunities. Collections opened up to new product categories and a new generation of designers that included names such as Ken Scott, Krizia, and Mila Schön. Fashion boutiques and sportswear gradually took precedence over high fashion. The fashion presented in Florence gradually differentiated itself from that proposed by the centres in Rome and Milan: the former being elitist, strongly anchored to the model of French *haute couture*, and the latter innovative in terms of materials but not designs. These were important achievements that once again confirmed Giorgini's ability to understand and interpret market trends. However, the foundations on which this process was built remained

[47] Pinchera (2009, 69).

fragile. The crisis of the municipal model of governance of Italian fashion that emerged in the late 1960s highlighted its contradictions. The Milanese CIM and the Roman CRAMI were also involved in this process. There was an imbalance between their strong local roots and their broader ambitions that led them to proclaim these cities capitals of Italian fashion. The limited sources of funding and the limited scope of action of the bodies involved in their foundation heavily influenced and directed their work and ambitions, irreversibly weakening their capacity to represent Italian fashion in a wider context.

2.3 The Business Interest Model: The AIIA

The *Associazione Italiana Industriali dell'Abbigliamento* (AIIA, Italian Clothing Industry Association) was the first business interest association (BIA) founded to safeguard the interests of the emerging Italian ready-to-wear industry. The functions of BIAs were primarily to provide bureaucratic support to their members and engage in lobbying activities to defend entrepreneurial interests. Throughout the twentieth century, BIAs gradually expanded their role, developing and surpassing the previously mentioned functions. The AIIA also followed this path, addressing issues related to the organization of the entire clothing production chain. Through the activity of the *Comitato Moda degli Industriali dell'Abbigliamento* (CMIA, Ready-to-Wear Fashion Council), the AIIA also dealt with managing the 'fashion variable,' an element which was crucial for the planning of the entire production cycle, yet rather volatile and particularly sensitive to social, economic, and cultural changes.

2.3.1 The First Ready-to-Wear Business Interest Association

The AIIA, set up in 1945, was the first business interest association (BIA) to protect the interests of the ready-to-wear industry. Historians and other social scientists have only recently and partially focused on these forms of business activity.[48] The interest of economic and business historians in BIAs is growing steadily.[49] Recent studies have highlighted their ability to increase the efficiency of the whole sector and to go beyond the interests of individual members, thus facilitating the process of economic development.[50]

The organization, development, and influence of BIAs and their political, social, and economic role can only become clear when the political, social, and economic context is fully understood.[51] As for the Italian context and the state of the Italian ready-to-wear industry at the end of World War II, the situation of the various players of the Italian fashion industry was rather complicated. In particular, the textile and clothing industries were faced with a shortfall in production infrastructure. The path to be followed was the increase in exports. To achieve this goal, it was necessary to improve both the quantity and quality of production. The diffusion and sharing of new skills and knowledge that this renewal involved created a strong stimulus for the foundation of an organization that, as well as protecting the interests of the ready-to-wear producers, could also help fulfil these needs.

The AIIA was founded in Milan just a few days after the end of World War II and was supported by the most authoritative representatives of all branches of the nascent ready-to-wear Italian industry, thus giving it the necessary authority to both perform the tasks and achieve the objectives listed in its statute.[52] The AIIA immediately joined *Confindustria* (the main Italian BIA). The objective was to make the ready-to-wear sector autonomous to gain more power for its lobbying activities. This autonomy took three directions. Firstly, from tailoring (artisan production) which had control of the *Federazione Nazionale Fascista dell'Abbigliamento* (National Fascist Clothing Federation, a trade association that

[48] See Galambos (1966), Feldman and Nocken (1975), Yamazaky and Miyamoto (1988), and Scranton (1998). We use the definition of BIAs as synonymous with industry, trade, profes sional, or employer associations, even though the most recent and updated studies in business and economic history indicate that there are some minor semantic differences between these definitions.

[49] Lanzalaco (2007, 298), Walker Laird (2008, 580–84).

[50] Doner and Schneider (2000) and Fraboulet-Rousselier et al. (2013).

[51] Feldman and Nocken (1975, 414–15).

[52] Paris (2021, 5–15).

included all parts of the Italian fashion industry).[53] Secondly, although some textile companies also continued to produce ready-made garments, the AIIA ratified the autonomy of the ready-to-wear industry from the textile industry. Thirdly, the creation of the AIIA separated ready-to-wear from knitwear and hosiery (a sector with a long tradition in Italy and its own BIA). The AIIA, therefore, marked a clear separation of artisanal production and industrial production also from the perspective of institutional representation. Moreover, again from the perspective of interest representation, it separated ready-to-wear from knitwear and textile. In this way, ready-to-wear companies had, for the first time, a tool at their disposal to protect the interests of the sector and strengthen their position within the emerging Italian fashion industry.

2.3.2 Organizational Structure and Activities

The organizational structure and the rules that drove the formation and management of government committees fully reflected the will of the AIIA to be wholly inclusive. First of all, towards the various branches of the ready-to-wear industry (from underwear to menswear and ladies' clothing), and secondly towards all subjects who were not part of the sector, but who could have been helpful in the pursuit of the statutory objectives. At the same time, the statute also protected smaller members, thanks to a voting system that limited the decision-making power of larger companies. Taking into account the needs of small and medium-sized enterprises was a decision that proved to be of particular importance in Italy, because they represented the foundation of the national manufacturing system, not only in clothing industries.[54] Even though the most productive regions for clothing were those in the northwest of the country, the composition of the Board of Management ensured adequate geographical representation within the management structures. The statutes also provided for a three-year term of office for positions of responsibility, and members were prohibited from joining associations or bodies in competition with the interests of the AIIA. In doing so, the AIIA sought to reduce the risk of early defection of members and to limit possible conflicts of interest, as well as the formation of internal lobbying

[53] Giulio Goehring (1961) and AIIA (1981).

[54] E.g., see Colli (2002).

groups. The organizational structure of the AIIA was, therefore, designed to meet the needs and represent the interests of all companies in the ready-to-wear industry, irrespective of their size, geographical location, or production specialization.

The statute also listed the actions that the AIIA should carry out in support of its individual members and to promote the development of the sector, thereby acting both as a network (internally) and as a node (externally). There were numerous goals to achieve, and the work of the AIIA extended beyond national borders. In this context, the AIIA contributed to the establishment of the European Association of Clothing Industry in 1947, aiming to participate in the development of the ready-to-wear industry at an international level. From this perspective, it became possible not only to exert a more influential lobbying effort at a European level, but also to closely study the main entrepreneurial experiences, share technical standards (particularly regarding product labelling and standardization of sizes), and gather information on foreign demand characteristics, with a view to increasing exports and exploiting the process of European integration.

The AIIA also carried out a wide range of market-complementing activities (supply of private goods) that, by reducing members' transaction costs, incentivized cooperation between companies and reinforced the role of the AIIA itself. These services ranged from assisting members participating in the most important Italian and foreign trade fairs, to supporting members with a constant supply of statistical and market data, collaboration with professional institutes for training courses, and tax and legal assistance. Cooperation, in this case, represented a strategic choice and was a consequence of the awareness of imperfections in the market.[55]

At the same time, the AIIA undertook a long series of market-supporting activities (supply of public goods) aimed at protecting and promoting the entire clothing sector. For example, it promoted exports thanks to close collaboration with the aforementioned ICE. The AIIA also obtained appreciable results in terms of import controls, above all for low-cost products from non-European countries that benefited from lower labour costs. This question was tackled at a national and international level by working with other European BIAs to define the best regulatory instruments for international commerce in textiles. This is the case for

[55] See Carnevali (2004).

the Multifiber Arrangement, which regulated international commerce of textile products and clothing until 2005, setting quotas for imports from developing countries.

Lobbying activity at a national and European level should not be overlooked and the AIIA achieved good results in this field also. The AIIA's significant participation in the *Comitato Consultivo della Moda* (Fashion Advisory Committee), initiated by the Ministry of Industry in 1967, was significant for its future.[56] Historical research has highlighted how the connections between BIAs and state or supra-state organizations could carry risks in terms of loss of autonomy and consequent dissatisfaction of members.[57] The objective of the Committee, placed under the guidance of the EIM, was to promote collaboration among the various parties which made up the production chain. The EIM represented political power in the Italian fashion world, and its support was particularly important in terms of promotion. The participation of the AIIA in the Committee was then necessary and fully aligned with its range of lobbying strategies.

2.3.3 Planning Fashion: The CMIA

Overall, the action of the AIIA can be viewed positively, at least until the mid-1960s. This is confirmed by the constant increase in the number of members. However, to assess the ability of BIAs to achieve their objectives, we must take into account not only the strength of their organizational structure, but also their capacity to adapt to the environment in which they operate. The changes in the economic, social, cultural, and institutional context, therefore, play an important role in their survival.[58]

As we have seen, the 1960s were characterized by a profound change in the demand for clothing. The entire fashion industry was forced to deal with a more diversified market, in which women and the younger generations were fully engaged in consumer mechanisms. The consequences were twofold. On the one hand, the emergence of new demand in terms of taste and price. On the other hand, a reversal of the entire cultural

[56] ASCNMI, b. 3, *Relazione del Consiglio direttivo all'Assemblea generale dei soci del 16 Dicembre 1967*; Comitato Consultivo della Moda (1969).

[57] E.g., see Svendsen (2014).

[58] Ville (2007, 298).

process of fashion: the reference point was no longer the high society lady, but the young dynamic woman.[59]

The so-called fashion risk was probably the factor that every ready-to-wear enterprise had to consider most. Fashion affected purchasing decisions and strongly influenced the entire production cycle. A survey conducted by DOXA (the first Italian statistical research and opinion survey company) in Western European countries between 1969 and 1970 highlighted, in particular, how more than half of the female respondents said they wore "the latest fashion" (a higher proportion than the male respondents). Italy showed one of the lowest percentages among major European countries, but more than a third of the Italian women interviewed (in line with the male respondents) claimed to follow fashion closely.[60] Fashion, therefore, was a double-edged sword: an enormous opportunity for those capable of mastering it, but a point of vulnerability for those unable to update their production strategies. The economic damage resulting from the rapid depreciation of fashion-influenced products was considered serious, and the most exposed enterprises were the larger companies. The increase in production scale and economies of scope that had facilitated their success in the 1950s had generated a structural rigidity (both technological and organizational) that jeopardized their survival. Finding the most suitable tools to mitigate such issues meant safeguarding the future of these enterprises at least, if not of the entire sector.

These changes had significant repercussions on the entire production chain. In this context, as mentioned in the first chapter, the price-quality ratio offered by Italian ready-to-wear firms was no longer sufficient. The action of the AIIA aimed to reorganize the entire production process more efficiently, starting from forecasting and supporting new fashion trends. Firstly, because some considered high fashion to be an outdated model. The new youth cultures, for example, sought their references elsewhere.[61] Additionally, the industry needed to plan production at least a year in advance of the release of new collections. This requirement did

[59] For more detail on the relationship between gender and consumption, also looking at the Italian case, see: De Grazia and Furlough (1996), Crane (2000), English (2007), Savage (2007), Liguori (1996), and Sassatelli (2006).

[60] AI (1971a).

[61] Polhemus (1994); on the Italian case see Paris (2010a).

not allow producers to wait for high fashion presentations, which took place only a few months before the market launch.

Ready-to-wear companies implemented two different strategies. Smaller and more flexible firms began to collaborate independently with young fashion designers. Larger companies, characterized by greater structural rigidity, instead opted for a path of centralized planning and control of fashion.[62] This dual approach highlighted the limited propensity for cooperation within the Italian ready-to-wear sector, further amplified by the impact of socio-economic changes on the organizational and technological structures of the companies. As observed in other creative industries, this division seemed to indicate that the association represented by the AIIA had perhaps never been the formal expression of an informal spirit of collaboration.[63]

The AIIA supported the second strategy (the planning of fashion) and the weight of the larger companies influenced this choice. The CMIA (Ready-to-wear Fashion Council) was established in 1959 by influential entrepreneurs belonging to the AIIA with precisely this objective in mind. The participation of companies such as Max Mara, Marzotto, and GFT, therefore, tilted the initiative towards the major producers (largely operating in the Milan-Turin axis), with the risk of compromising not only the CMIA's activities, but also those of the AIIA.

In coordination with other similar international bodies under the supervision of the European Association of Clothing Industry, the CMIA was tasked with defining the materials, colours, and model lines as references for new collections, with sufficient lead time to allow companies to plan their entire production cycle. The CMIA was also responsible for implementing various actions aimed at informing and guiding the market (from retailers to the media and even consumers), including organizing dedicated events.[64] The CMIA was therefore operating as a mediator rather than as a simple predictor of fashion.

The initial results regarding colours definition were achieved in the mid-1960s and received a positive response from industry professionals.[65]

[62] Legnazzi (1960).

[63] Popp (2005).

[64] Confezione (1969).

[65] E.g., see Legnazzi (1963) and Goehring (1969).

However, there was a hidden negative aspect that was totally overlooked. With these agreements, larger companies relinquished some of their decision-making autonomy to third parties in exchange for a reduction of risk connected with the variability of fashion. This choice did not prevent a crisis in the ready-to-wear sector. The creative phase was crucial for the whole production process. Delegating this function to other bodies removed an important tool for market competition and differentiation from the hands of ready-to-wear companies. The true role of fashion councils was then to make up for the lack of the creative phase within many of the largest clothing companies.[66] Instead, the best way to develop the creative phase was to establish the best conditions for it to flourish.[67]

Evaluating the impact of CMIA initiatives is complex, mainly due to the lack of archival sources. While the press served as an informative tool, fully assessing the contribution it made to the CMIA's objectives is challenging. Estimating the impact of numerous events directly organized by the CMIA is even more difficult. The support provided to member companies seeking participation in specialized markets such as SAMIA may have been more beneficial for the promotion of individual companies rather than for the advancement of the CMIA's objectives.

However, some additional observations can be made regarding the ability to influence consumer choices. Understanding the factors that most influenced consumers was essential not only at a wider level for promoting seasonal materials and colours, but also at the individual company level to identify target markets and optimize the entire production cycle, along with distribution and promotional strategies. In the mid-1960s, both the press and fashion shows represented two instruments which were significantly influencing consumer decisions, but they were not the only factors and, for certain consumer categories, not even the most important. While some studies confirm that fashion played an increasingly important role in buying decisions, it also emerged that such trends had a more significant impact on women and younger consumers, who regarded fashion as more than just a matter of clothing.

Instead, the street was the main source of information for those whose interest in fashion was considered marginal. Consulting the press also

[66] Paris (2021, 15–18).

[67] Pouillard (2016).

played a role, but it did not involve specialized publications invested in by the CMIA. Television, shop windows, fashion shows, and the choices of VIPs (actors, singers, and celebrities in general) followed as other sources of influence. It is worth noting that all these tools held strictly informative value because, when it came to making actual purchase decisions, people looked at what was displayed in the shop windows of major stores, guaranteeing fashion that was not only advertised but also effectively worn. Thus, the choices of the CMIA seem to confirm a partial lack of understanding of the ongoing changes in Italian society.

The initiatives of the CMIA achieved some positive results, but by the end of the 1960s, it was clear that the simple strategy of planning was not sufficient. The ready-to-wear industry had to go further, essentially retracing its steps and reintroducing the old theme of coordination: upstream with the creative phase and downstream with distribution.

The challenge for the AIIA and the CMIA was, therefore, to create a genuine 'system'. However, a second miscalculation was on the horizon. The work carried out in collaboration with other institutions such as the CNMI reflected the idea of a hierarchical fashion system for the creative phase (with the top *couturier(e)s* at the summit) and a dualistic system for the structure of production and target markets (tailoring on the one side and large-scale industry for the mass market on the other). This concept was overtaken by the reality of the facts, but it still led the main institutions involved to pursue general sectoral agreements rather than allowing individual companies to act freely. The role of supervisor that the EIM still held in this institutional scheme probably also influenced the choice of this strategy. The EIM, in fact, continued to push for coordination between high fashion and industry, always to be accomplished at an institutional level.

The High Fashion and Ready-to-wear Industry Arrangement (*Accordo Alta Moda-Industria*) signed in 1971 by the EIM, the CNMI, and the AIIA, among others, is emblematic of this situation. Collaboration was undoubtedly more efficient than planning, and coordination among the various components of Italian fashion was a priority, but it had to take place at the level of individual companies and not through top-down agreements which were difficult to implement at the level of individual producers. There were too many variables to take into account when planning the production cycle effectively. Each company had to analyse all of these factors in order to best adapt them to its own situation and independently find its ideal position within the market, matching its structure to the most suitable market strategy. In this new context, the role of the various BIAs also would have to be reconsidered.

Under these conditions, the High Fashion and Ready-to-wear Arrangement was also bound to fail. From this situation, companies that individually developed the correct relationship between creation, production, and distribution emerged. These were small and medium-sized enterprises (SMEs) capable of skilfully combining the constraints of mass production with the tastes of the public and the increasingly rapid changes in fashion. These flexible businesses were able to benefit from a cost structure that also allowed them to efficiently produce small, constantly renewed collections sold in exclusive stores (so-called boutique shops).[68] In this way, it became possible to shorten the production cycle, reduce delivery times, and carry less stock, thus adapting with greater agility to market variations. Collaborating with young fashion designers who catered for their peers also allowed the tastes of a new, important, and dynamic market segment to be captured.

These companies represented the new vanguard of the industry and, due to their influence on the market, quickly became leading players in the Italian ready-to-wear industry. In the early 1970s, the AIIA was fully aware of this situation as it excluded such firms. The AIIA deemed them dangerous for all those companies that were unable to maintain the same performance levels. With this attitude, the AIIA proved that it represented only a portion of the sector, and not even the best performing part. Therefore, the failure of the AIIA was twofold, as it failed to attract the smaller, more dynamic enterprises and, at the same time, it was unable to protect the larger, struggling companies.[69] Therefore, the AIIA represented an outdated way of viewing and organizing the textile and clothing supply chain, which historical companies—those that had contributed to the sector's success until at least the mid-1960s and still held the reins of the AIIA—were unwilling (or unable) to relinquish.

There are two closely interrelated reasons for the failure of the AIIA. The first was the lack of organizational flexibility, which kept it firmly in the hands of the larger enterprises and their owners, some of whom were also founding members. Giulio Goehring of the Milanese Fabbrica Italiana Biancheria epitomizes this situation, as he held the important

[68] Fogg (2003) and Chevalier (2007).

[69] On business failure see Fridenson (2004, 567–78) and Van Rooij (2014).

position of President from 1945 to 1973. According to some studies on creative industries, however, in such situations, some responsibility also lies with smaller enterprises, which tend to be particularly resistant to calls for unity.[70] This is true also for the Italian ready-to-wear industry.[71] Some surveys carried out during the 1970s seem to confirm both theories.[72] The lack of pluralism was indeed considered the main cause of dissatisfaction with the BIAs, not only within the fashion industry but also outside the sector. Within the fashion industry, however, the ready-to-wear sector recorded one of the highest rates of discontent. This meant that not all the AIIA members were open to dialogue and discussion on the key issues under consideration.

The interviewees also accused the BIAs of not fully understanding the ongoing economic and social changes, thus rendering them unable to provide adequate guidance on the main problems to be addressed and the resulting policies to be adopted. The second reason for the failure of the AIIA is closely related to this aspect. The enterprises worst affected by this attitude were, naturally, the larger firms that were more exposed to the winds of change. These were the companies that needed answers most, as they were experiencing a severe crisis, and only some would re-emerge in the late 1970s—also due to their collaboration with a new generation of fashion designers who managed all phases of the production process. It was, therefore, the fashion designers who succeeded where the AIIA and CMIA had failed, domesticating the phenomenon of fashion to finally build a new and internationally competitive fashion system. This challenge tested the structural rigidity of the major clothing producers, but it paved the way for a new phase of development in the sector.

By the mid-1970s, the AIIA was no longer able to protect the interests of a sector that had witnessed the failure of many important companies. The negotiations for the renewal of national collective labour contracts presented an opportunity to establish, together with other BIAs, a new trade association capable of bringing together, coordinating, protecting, and promoting the interests of all the enterprises of the various branches of the textile and clothing industry. In 1975, the *Federazione*

[70] Popp (2005, 1846–47).

[71] E.g., see Piccoli (1970).

[72] Ciabattoni (1976, 70–81).

tra le Associazioni delle Industrie Tessili e dell'Abbigliamento (*Federtessile*, Federation of Associations of Textile and Clothing Industries) was born. The challenge was no longer solely economic. Fashion was one of the most economically significant sectors of the country, but also an important cultural industry which needed a new approach and a renewed institutional organization.

2.4 The Hierarchical Model: The CNMI

A decade of institutional effervescence followed the birth of Italian fashion, which fashion historians unanimously trace back to 1951, the year when the first Italian Fashion Show of genuine Italian collections was held in *Palazzo Pitti* in Florence. Throughout the 1950s, there were various attempts to counteract the success and autonomy of Florence. As a result, in the early 1960s there was still no institutional body capable of representing Italian fashion on a national scale. In an effort to fill the institutional vacuum, and to overcome conflicts and contrasts, the CNMI was founded in 1962.

2.4.1 The CNMI Before the CNMI

Although the debut of Italian fashion on the international stage in 1951 was a significant event for the future of Italian fashion, the catwalks of Florence were far from being a real launch pad for Italy to achieve a position alongside and on a par with the dominant players in the international fashion market. Thanks to Giorgini, Italian fashion gained international recognition for the first time in its history during the 1950s. The quality and taste of Italian production were beyond question, and its competitiveness was ensured by labour costs well below those of any other industrialized country. However, in terms of sizes and production techniques, Italian exports were based on artisanal production, mainly of accessories and knitwear. The success of Florence and its limitations made it evident that the lack of an institutional body capable of representing Italian fashion as a whole was a problem whose solution could not be further postponed.

Some years after the debut of Italian fashion on the international stage, Giorgini himself promoted the establishment of the *Camera Sindacale della Moda Italiana* (Chamber of Italian Fashion), which was founded in 1958 by *couturier(e)s* such as Maria Antonelli, Roberto Capucci, Princess

Giovanna Caracciolo Ginetti, Alberto Fabiani and his wife Simonetta Colonna Romano Di Cesarò, Cesare Guidi, Germana Marucelli, Emilio Schuberth, and Jole Veneziani—all of whom had accepted Giorgini's invitation to the fashion shows held in Florence in 1951. Giorgini took on the role of President. The *Camera Sindacale* began to operate in 1962, after a long gestation period, and with the new name of the *Camera Nazionale della Moda Italiana*. In the meantime, individual and collective initiatives, more or less intentionally aimed at defending the prerogatives of urban centres vying for the role of Italian fashion capital, hindered any attempt to provide Italian fashion with a unified institutional body.

As we have seen, the *Camera Sindacale* was just the latest addition to a series of associations formed in the previous decade. Since the early 1950s, their coexistence had not been peaceful. In 1951, the CIM and the EIM, based in Turin, established the Italian Fashion Service with the aim of jointly regulating, coordinating, and organizing fashion shows. Industrialists such as Marinotti and Marzotto sponsored the initiative, but it failed in its attempt to challenge the autonomy of Florence. In 1953, prominent *couturier(e)s* from Rome—Fabiani, Simonetta, Schuberth, the Sorelle Fontana, Ferdinandi, and Garnett—founded the *Sindacato Italiano dell'Alta Moda* (Italian High Fashion Syndicate), later renamed the CRAMI, and began showcasing their collections in their own ateliers in Rome, two days before the Florentine presentations. Reasons for dissatisfaction were both Giorgini's focus on boutique fashion and accessories and the "collective" formula of the Florentine shows. It was believed that the former distracted the attention of buyers and the press from high fashion proposals. The latter allowed foreign buyers to compare fashion collections at a glance thus making the audience's occasional lack of enthusiasm for some proposals visible to rivals.

In short, Italian fashion was still without a governing system when Paris—the undisputed arbiter of taste and, above all, the fashion show calendar—decided to bring forward its own shows by a few days, forcing Florence to do the same and thus giving Rome a very narrow window in which to organize its own events. The inevitable overlaps that would occur intensified the problem of managing the show calendar and increased awareness of the urgency to establish a coordinating body. In 1960, the CRAMI proposed an agreement to the Florentine CFMI, which served as the foundation for the revival of the idea of creating a unified body, the CNMI.

At the end of 1960, an assembly was convened in Rome for the renewal of positions and the formulation of a programme for fashion events. The assembly marked only a temporary interruption of the inactivity that had characterized the first two years of the *Camera Sindacale*'s existence, and this inertia continued. The reasons for this inaction can only be reconstructed through articles by authoritative figures in the fashion press, but these sources are inherently journalistic in nature. The speculation ranged from national sabotage to international conspiracies, while more plausible explanations included long-standing personal and institutional rivalries. Objectively, the group of founders, composed of prominent Roman *couturier(e)s*, and the influence exerted by the CRAMI led the *Camera Sindacale* to be heavily biased towards high fashion. Other product categories and related production activities remained on the periphery of the scope of the newly-established association.

2.4.2 Organizational Structure and Activities

It is interesting to note that the CNMI's statute was modelled on the statute of the *Chambre sindicale de la couture Parisienne*, established in 1868. A typed copy of the French association's statute, accompanied by handwritten annotations, is preserved in the historical archive of its Italian counterpart.

The statute, approved in 1962, reaffirmed the original purpose of *Camera Sindacale*: to coordinate various initiatives aimed at promoting Italian fashion and to collaborate with both political institutions and private organizations. Consistent with its statutory purpose, the regulations emphasized the objective of "establishing a systematic organization and, therefore, controlling the work activities carried out in the fashion sector" through the introduction of trade registers for the following categories: high fashion houses, fashion tailors, boutique fashion creators, garment manufacturers, furriers, fashion houses, and fashion accessory businesses, while specifying the necessary requirements for entry.

The strong similarities—starting from the names of the two associations—between the French and Italian statutes and regulations demonstrate that, despite the fact that in the early 1960s Paris's role as the undisputed arbiter of European taste may have begun to fade in the eyes of Italian *couturier(e)s*, the French capital was more than ever a model to imitate in terms of organization, coordination, and regulation of various fashion-related activities, from the training of workers to the marketing of accessories and clothing, from manufacturing to branding, from fashion shows to advertising.

The initiative to set up an organization similar to that which had been operating in France for almost a century was a clear sign of the awareness that Italian fashion had nothing to envy in terms of creativity and tailoring skills when compared to French fashion. Instead, its weaknesses were to be found elsewhere, namely in the extreme fragmentation of promotional initiatives that were meant to give Italian fashion resonance, in the backwardness of the educational system that should have provided a constant supply of new technical and creative resources, in the impromptu relationship with textile producers, in the relatively low per capita income that prevented it from growing within a prosperous domestic market, and, not least, in the institutional vacuum.

The statute, however, is just the first in a series of historical sources preserved in the CNMI archive, whose nature and quantity indicate that the CNMI was significantly different from existing fashion centres in terms of size and scope. Firstly, primary sources reveal how inclusive the organizational structure of the CNMI was. Historical sources regarding members of the CNMI highlight numerous entities and organizations already operating in the fashion world that the CNMI explicitly recognized, committing not to interfere, limit, or modify their prerogatives and competencies. The archival documentation also provides evidence of the breadth of CNMI's institutional scope. Membership, for instance, was open to all Italian chambers of commerce. The list of members includes all types of fashion-related manufacturers. The organizational structure included the board of directors, whose members were elected by the general assembly of the CNMI and designated by the executive committees, whose members were representatives of the professional categories regulated by the CNMI.

Almost all existing centres became members of the CNMI. However, this does not mean that the aforementioned entities immediately accepted the CNMI. The EIM, for example, engaged in a prolonged campaign to limit its power, claiming exclusive rights to represent all of Italian fashion at a governmental level.[73] The issue of coordinating the fashion show calendar fuelled controversies throughout the 1960s and beyond. In an attempt to bring order to such a contentious matter, in 1967

[73] Paris (2006, 237–41).

the Chamber announced the decision to separate the management of the Florentine fashion show calendar from the organization of the Roman fashion shows and prepared the last unified calendar for both events. Predictably, the majority of fashion houses supported this decision. However, the EIM disapproved, as the change further marginalized Turin. Buyers and the foreign press were rather sceptical. Equally thorny was the issue of classifying and regulating the activities that composed the ever more multifaceted world of fashion. The resolution of the CNMI's board of directors in 1971, which established the new sector of ready-to-wear *haute couture*, sparked a predictably indignant and concerned reaction from the Florentine CFMI, whose President—Franco Tancredi—demanded clarification on "what is intended to change by setting up the sector of ready-to-wear *haute couture* creators when such a sector already existed, albeit under a French name".

The primary sources kept in the CNMI archive provide a wealth of information on CNMI activities, particularly those of the 1960s. These initiatives only seemed to overlap with those of the EIM. Unlike the EIM, the CNMI was, in fact, a trade association. Therefore, when engaged in external activities, the CNMI primarily spoke on behalf of its members, aiming to represent the Italian fashion industry as a whole. The documentation describes the keen participation in conferences in Italy and abroad, the advocacy efforts to raise awareness among political authorities of the importance of fashion for the Italian economy, leading to the establishment of the *Comitato Consultivo della Moda*, and the agreements reached with private industrial partners such as Rhodiatoce and Lanerossi. However, the majority of primary sources relate to foreign and Italian Fashion Shows. The CNMI was constantly in contact with the aforementioned ICE, consulates, embassies, and the specialized press, with the dual intentions of acquiring information about foreign fashion shows to share with its members, and establishing channels for the promotion of Italian fashion abroad. With regard to Italian Fashion Shows, the archival documentation demonstrates the growing complexity of administrative, accounting, advertising, and technical aspects related to show organization, which over time had been built around key activities such as preparing the fashion show calendar, preparing accompanying material for the presentation of individual collections, managing relationships with suppliers, the press, and buyers, and collecting press reviews. The CNMI maintained contacts with a variety of stakeholders involved in the shows, aiming to activate every promotional channel and ensure the attendance at shows of the specialized press, institutions, and the business community.

Such a rich collection of historical documentation allows us to better understand the distinctive features that strongly differentiate the fashion shows in Florence from those organized in Rome, starting with the venue, the Campidoglio Palace, one of the symbols of Roman political power. To consolidate and highlight the connection with the political sphere, some of the most important national political figures were invited to the opening ceremony of the high fashion shows. On these occasions, the vision that the government bodies had of the fashion industry became clear. In 1967, for example, the Minister of Industry, Giulio Andreotti, a prominent figure in Italian political history in the second half of the twentieth century, emphasized that fashion was not just a symbol of the ephemeral and frivolous. By looking at the economic data of the sector and the ripple effects generated solely by fashion shows, it was evident that fashion was much more, starting from its economic relevance. Moreover, for Minister Andreotti, a member of the main Italian political party (Christian Democratic Party), fashion also had a higher function, namely to express the "will and moral direction" of a country.[74] For these reasons, Andreotti promised that all necessary actions would be taken to support the sector. The list of commitments was extensive and included, among other things, the establishment of a commission to align Italian legislation on model protection with the rules set by the Hague Convention in 1960, the regulation of professional apprenticeships, and above all, the renewal of funding for high fashion houses (increased from 37 million ITL in 1963 to 86 million ITL in 1966). There was also a pledge to establish the *Comitato Consultivo della Moda*, tasked with preparing a "guidance" document for public administration and private operators to present to the Inter-ministerial Committee for Economic Planning.

The political and institutional agenda was therefore full of commitments ranging from the legal domain to that of education, from coordinating public and private initiatives for the promotion of the sector to defining its directions of development. It was essential not to lose sight of the common guiding principle behind such a wide range of actions. At the conclusion of his speech, the Minister explicitly referred to a fashion magazine that had published "models entirely in tune with those of the

[74] ASCNMI, b. 168, f. 168-2, *Comunicato stampa*.

so-called bourgeois countries". As the magazine in question was Soviet, a notable detail in the context of the international political climate marked by the intensification of the Cold War, the reproduction of Western models was considered highly positive. This indicated that for the Italian government, fashion not only had economic and moral value, but also political significance. Given that Andreotti's speech was delivered during the time of Mary Quant's revolution, and as the Minister held decision-making power regarding public funding for private production activities, including fashion houses, it sounded like a stern warning to Italian fashion creators not to imitate such subversive examples. The historical documentation related to the Autumn–Winter 1967 fashion show allows us to understand how the creators effectively interpreted the strongly conservative moral and political value attributed to fashion, using the shows as a means to communicate it to a wide-ranging audience (in Rome, 200 buyers and 300 journalists were present, representing 200 publications from 25 different countries).

On the Roman catwalks, 3,500 models created by 50 fashion houses were paraded. At the end of the event, the CNMI took the initiative to issue an informative statement, highlighting not only the extremely positive figures but also commenting on the trends emerging from the models presented. The CNMI emphasized how the "new" Italian fashion had "drastically abandoned Beat influences, condemning the miniskirt to death" and returning "to the traditional, romantic cut of garments". Rather provocatively, considering the broader context, the *total look* was inspired by a return to the past. Women were free to choose how to dress, but it was noted that 1968 would be "the year of the woman who [...] could barely tolerate the Beat or yé-yé style". Revivals prevailed in clothing and accessories, such as hats, socks, and shoes. Revivals were also popular in men's fashion, which was expected to boom.[75]

By the end of the 1960s, Italian high fashion boasted of being focused on the past rather than being ahead of the times. With this inability to reinterpret the past in a modern context, to "provide new answers to new questions", high fashion suffered a "loss of beauty" that visually represented the reasons for its crisis.[76] High fashion's main antagonist

[75] ASCNMI, b. 168, f. 168-1, *Nota riassuntiva sulla manifestazione dell'alta moda italiana per l'autunno-inverno 1967–68.*

[76] Butazzi (1987, 9) and Olivari Binaghi (1996, 529).

was ready-to-wear, which, born from a process of impoverishment of high fashion, not only stole the spotlight but also the ability to influence aesthetic choices.[77] The challenges faced by high fashion were not unique to Italy; they affected the entire sector across Europe. However, by the late 1960s, no signs of this change were evident on the Roman catwalks. Giorgini, on the other hand, had grasped and embraced this change in Florence, where he presented ready-to-wear models under the name of *alta moda pronta*. Yet, he would not be able to further develop this concept due to the lack of an appropriate production structure.

During the 1970s, the emergence of Milan as an international fashion hub found the CNMI unprepared to promptly recognize and manage the fashion revolution which was occurring at the time. Notably, it was only by the late 1980s that CNMI's headquarters relocated from Rome to Milan, and a new generation of CNMI presidents, coming from the fashion business world, replaced the previous incumbents, who were representatives of political parties. These included the Deputy (1958–1963), Minister (1981–1982), and Senator (1992–1994) Luciano Radi (member of the Christian Democrats party); Giorgio Zicari the journalist, secret service informant and P2 Masonic Lodge member; and Vittorio Barattieri an exponent of the Republican Party who, as Director General for Industrial Production, oversaw the allocation of billions of lire to companies.

To recap, primary sources allow us to recognize that the issue of coordinating the calendar of fashion shows and the related issue of classifying and regulating the activity of those who were admitted to them remained central to the CNMI's history, eventually shaping its governance model as hierarchical, being centred on high fashion as the top-ranking fashion category. The CNMI was an association created by *couturier(e)s* who, like their French counterparts in the nineteenth-century, considered themselves outstanding creative geniuses. The primary purpose of the CNMI was to coordinate the various promotional initiatives aimed at promoting Italian high fashion rather than the entire Italian fashion industry. Additionally, the CNMI's statute explicitly recognized the need for greater collaboration with both political institutions and private organizations representing industrial, artisanal, commercial, and professional categories

[77] Fiorentini Capitani (1991, 13).

to more effectively manage issues of mutual interest. Essentially, coordination was an internal matter for the association, whereas collaboration involved the relationships between the association and the public and private actors who, to varying degrees and with different objectives and roles, were interested in capitalizing on the favourable outcomes achieved by Giorgini's initiative. Consistent with this belief, the CNMI sought to implement a hierarchical model of governance on the fashion system in which high fashion occupied the top position. Historical sources show an anachronistically complete adoption of the French institutional model by the CNMI. Conservatism characterized the CNMI's actions, ultimately resulting in its inability to manage the transition from high fashion to ready-to-wear fashion, condemning the Italian unified body to repeated attempts to make ready-to-wear the cornerstone of Italian fashion without questioning the supremacy of high fashion.

References

AIIA. 1981. *Cento domande, una sola risposta: Associazione Italiana Industriali Abbigliamento*. Milan: AIIA.

Bertilorenzi, Marco, Cerretano, Valerio, and Mario Perugini. 2022. "Between Constraints and Opportunities: Big Italian Business and Autarky, 1934–1943." *Rivista di storia economica* 38 (3): 303–36.

Bottero, Amelia. 1979. *Nostra signora la moda*. Milan: Mursia.

Butazzi, Grazietta. 1987. "Prefazione." In *La moda italiana*, vol. I, *Le origini dell'alta moda e la maglieria*, edited by G. Butazzi and A. Mottola Molfino, 7–10. Milan: Electa.

Capalbo, Cinzia. 2012. *Storia della moda a Roma. Sarti, culture e stili di una capitale dal 1871 a oggi*. Rome: Donzelli.

Carnevali, Francesca. 2004. "Crooks, Thieves, and Receivers: Transaction Costs in Nineteenth-Century Industrial Birmingham." *Economic History Review* 57 (3): 533–50.

Cerretano, Valerio. 2020. "Autarky, Market Creation and Innovation: Snia Viscosa and Saici, 1933–70." *Business History* 64 (6): 1110–30.

Chevalier, Gérald. 2007. "La boutique des années 1960: un nouvel espace pour un nouveau mode de consommation." In *La mode des Sixties. L'entreé dans a modernité*, edited by D. Veillon and M. Ruffat, 193–201. Paris: Autrement.

Ciabattoni, Amos. 1976. *Il sistema moda*. Turin: Editoriale Valentino.

Coleman, William D., and Henry J. Jacek. 1983. "The Roles and Activities of Business Interest Associations in Canada." *Canadian Journal of Political Science* 16 (2): 257–80.

Colli, Andrea. 2002. *I volti di Proteo. Storia della piccola impresa in Italia nel Novecento.* Turin: Bollati Boringhieri.
Colli, Andrea. 2003. "Fibre chimiche." In *La moda. Storia d'Italia. Annali 19*, edited by C. M. Belfanti and F. Giusberti, 483–521. Turin: Einaudi.
Collicelli Cagol, Stefano. 2008. *Venezia e la vitalità del contemporaneo. Paolo Marinotti a Palazzo Grassi (1959–1967).* Padua: il Poligrafo.
Comitato Consultivo della Moda. 1969. *Atti del Comitato Consultivo della Moda.* Turin: EIM.
Confezione. 1969. "Comitato moda degli industriali dell'abbigliamento italiano." *Confezione Italiana*, October–December 1969, n.p.
Crane, Diana. 2000. *Fashion and Its Social Agendas: Class, Gender and Identity in Clothing.* Chicago: University of Chicago Press.
De Grazia, Victoria, and Ellen Furlough, eds. 1996. *The Sex of Things: Gender and Consumption in Historical Prospective.* Berkeley: University of California Press.
De Marly, Diana. 1980. *The History of Haute Couture (1850–1950).* New York: Holmnes & Meier.
Di Castro, Federica, ed. 1991. *1900–1960 l'alta moda capitale. Torino e le sartorie torinesi.* Milan: Fabbri, Bompiani, Sonzogno, Etas.
Di Martino, Paolo, and Michelangelo Vasta, eds. 2017. *Ricchi per caso. La parabola dello sviluppo economico italiano.* Bologna: Mulino.
Doner, Richard F., and Ben Schneider. 2000. "Business Associations and Economic Development: Why Some Associations Contribute More Than Others." *Business and Politics* 2 (3): 261–88.
English, Bonnie. 2007. *A Cultural History of Fashion in the 20th Century.* Oxford: Berg.
Ente Italiano della Moda. 1966a. *Statuto 1966.* Turin: EIM.
Ente Italiano della Moda. 1966b. *Torino e l'abbigliamento.* Turin: EIM.
Feldman, Gerald D., and Ulrich Nocken. 1975. "Trade Associations and Economic Power: Interest Group Development in the Iron and Steel and Machines Building Industries, 1900–1933." *Business History Review* 49 (4): 413–45.
Ferretti, Roberto. 2011. "L'Iri durante il fascismo: struttura organizzativa, burocrazia e prassi amministrativa." *Amministrare* 19 (1): 123–225.
Fiorentini Capitani, Aurora. 1991. *Moda italiana: anni cinquanta e sessanta.* Florence: Cantini.
Fogg, Marnie. 2003. *Boutique: A '60s Cultural Phenomenon.* London: Mitchell Beazley.
Fraboulet-Rousselier, Danièle, Andrea Maria Locatelli, and Paolo Tedeschi, eds. 2013. *Historical and International Comparison of Business Interest Associations, 19th–20th Centuries.* Brussels: Peter Lang.

Fridenson, Patrick. 2004. "Business Failure and the Agenda of Business History." *Enterprise & Society* 5 (4): 562–82.
Galambos, Louis. 1966. *Competition and Cooperation: The Emergence of a National Trade Association*. Baltimore, MD: Johns Hopkins University Press.
Giras. 1969. "Le *nozze d'argento* del MITAM." *L'Abbigliamento Italiano* 11 (6) (June): 2, 18.
Gnoli, Sofia. 2000. *La donna, l'eleganza, il fascismo. La Moda Italiana dalle origini all'Ente Nazionale della Moda*. Catania: Prisma.
Gnoli, Sofia. 2014. *The Origins of Italian Fashion: 1900–45*. London: Victoria and Albert Museum.
Goehring, Giulio. 1961. "L'industria della confezione in Italia." In AIIA, *Guida della confezione*, 12–22, Milan: AIIA.
Goehring, Giulio. 1969. "Prevedere la moda senza snaturarla." *Confezione Italiana*, October–December, 3.
Grau, Francoise Marie. 2000. *La haute couture*. Paris: PUF.
John, Richard R., and Kim Phillips-Fein, eds. 2007. *Capital Gains: Business and Politics in Twentieth-Century America*. Philadelphia: University of Pennsylvania Press.
L'Abbigliamento Italiano. 1959a. "Abbiamo letto per voi…" *L'Abbigliamento Italiano* 1 (2) (July): 6.
L'Abbigliamento Italiano. 1959b. "Ai margini della moda." *L'Abbigliamento Italiano* 1 (4) (September): 6.
L'Abbigliamento Italiano. 1959c. "L'EIM riprende la sua attività." *L'Abbigliamento Italiano* 1 (4) (September): 6.
L'Abbigliamento Italiano. 1960a. "L'Ente Italiano della Moda riprende la sua attività." *L'Abbigliamento Italiano* 2 (1) (January): 1, 9.
L'Abbigliamento Italiano. 1960b. "L'abbigliamento italiano sul mercato Sudafricano." *L'Abbigliamento Italiano* 2 (1) (January): 5.
L'Abbigliamento Italiano. 1960c. "Lo Statuto dell'Ente Italiano della Moda." *L'Abbigliamento Italiano* 2 (1) (January): 2, 4.
L'Abbigliamento Italiano. 1960d. "La moda italiana nel Sud Africa [1]." *L'Abbigliamento Italiano* 2 (2) (February): 2.
L'Abbigliamento Italiano. 1960e. "L'Assemblea generale ordinaria dell'EIM." *L'Abbigliamento Italiano* 2 (3) (March): 2.
L'Abbigliamento Italiano. 1960f. "La moda italiana nel Sud Africa [2]." *L'Abbigliamento Italiano* 2 (3) (March): 5.
L'Abbigliamento Italiano. 1960h. "Notiziario dell'Ente Italiano della Moda." *L'Abbigliamento Italiano* 2 (10) (October): 21.
L'Abbigliamento Italiano. 1960i. "Due riunioni del Consiglio Generale dell'EIM." *L'Abbigliamento Italiano* 2 (12) (December): 15.
L'Abbigliamento Italiano. 1962a. "Notiziario dell'Ente Italiano della Moda." *L'Abbigliamento Italiano* 4 (4) (May–June): 12–14.

L'Abbigliamento Italiano. 1962c. "L'Ente Italiano della Moda alla Mostra italiana di Amburgo." *L'Abbigliamento Italiano* 3 (6) (November–December): 19.
L'Abbigliamento Italiano. 1966. "Dieci anni di sviluppi tessili." *L'Abbigliamento Italiano* 8 (4) (April): 1, 4.
L'Abbigliamento Italiano. 1969a. "In apertura di Moda-Selezione." *L'Abbigliamento Italiano* 11 (4) (April): 1.
L'Abbigliamento Italiano. 1969b. "Elenco delle case partecipanti alla rassegna mercato Moda Selezione 1." *L'Abbigliamento Italiano* 11 (4) (April): 5.
L'Abbigliamento Italiano. 1969c. "Anche il *Samia* sulla cresta dell'onda." *L'Abbigliamento Italiano* 11 (5) (May): 1.
L'Abbigliamento Italiano. 1969d. "A Torino la *maturità* per la confezione di lusso italiana." *L'Abbigliamento Italiano* 11 (5) (May): 1, 24.
L'Abbigliamento Italiano. 1970. "La nuova direzione dell'Ente Italiano della Moda." *L'Abbigliamento Italiano* X12 (9) (September): 3, 35.
L'Abbigliamento Italiano. 1971a. "Atteggiamenti verso la moda." *L'Abbigliamento Italiano* 13 (1) (January): 11.
L'Abbigliamento Italiano. 1971b. "Riunione dell'Assemblea Generale dei Soci dell'Ente Italiano della Moda." *L'Abbigliamento Italiano* 13 (4) (April): 7.
L'Abbigliamento Italiano. 1971c. "Il nuovo Statuto dell'Ente Italiano della Moda." *L'Abbigliamento Italiano* 13 (14) (December 15–30): 5.
L'Abbigliamento Italiano. 1972. "La nuova struttura dell'EIM è una realtà. Approvata la riforma statutaria." *L'Abbigliamento Italiano* 14 (9) (May): 4.
Lanzalaco, Luca. 2007. "Business Interest Associations." In *The Oxford Handbook of Business History*, edited by G. Jones and J. Zeitlin, 293–315. Oxford: Oxford University Press.
Lavanga, Mariangela. 2018. "The Role of Pitti Uomo Trade Fair in the Menswear Fashion Industry." In *The Fashion Forecasters: A Hidden History of Color and Trend Prediction*, edited by R. Blaszczyk and B. Wubs, 191–209. London: Bloomsbury Academic Publishing.
Legnazzi, Milo E. 1960. "Pianificazione e coordinamento della moda su larga base." *L'Abbigliamento Italiano* 2 (11) (November): 8.
Legnazzi, Milo E. 1963. "Il coordinamento internazionale dei colori di moda diventa realtà." *L'Abbigliamento Italiano*, September–October: 13.
Liguori, Maria Chiara. 1996. "Donne e consumi nell'Italia degli anni Cinquanta." *Italia Contemporanea* (205): 665–89.
Linea. 1955. "Da Milano." *Linea. Rivista dell'alta moda*, Spring Edition.
Linea. 1961. "Nel repertorio della confezione." *Linea. Rivista dell'alta moda*, Winter Edition.
Lipovetsky, Gilles. 1987. *L'empire de l'éphèmere*. Paris: Gallimard.
Lupano, Mario, and Alessandra Vaccari, eds. 2009. *Fashion at the Time of Fascism*. Bologna: Damiani.

Marroncini, L. 1972. "Dal Valentino uno scossone nell'importante settore della moda italiana." *Produttività* 3 (March): 180–81.

Misia. 1957. "Successo del primo MITAM". *Linea. Rivista dell'alta moda*, Autumn Edition: 58.

Nocentini, Sara. 2005a. "Alle origini dell'Istituto Nazionale per il Commercio Estero." *Passato e Presente* 3: 65–89.

Nocentini, Sara. 2005b. "L'ICE e la distribuzione degli aiuti post bellici in Italia (1943–1950)." *Studi Storici* 1: 155–86.

Nocentini, Sara. 2007. "L'Ice dalla Ricostruzione ai primi anni Settanta. Appunti per una ricerca storica." In *L'Italia nell'economia internazionale. Rapporto Ice 2006–2007*, edited by ICE, 524–31. Rome: ICE.

Olivari Binaghi, Maria Teresa. 1996. "La moda: le tendenze." In *Storia di Milano. Il Novecento*, vol. XVIII, t. 3, 496–563. Rome: Istituto della Enciclopedia Italiana Treccani.

Paris, Ivan. 2006. *Oggetti cuciti. L'abbigliamento pronto in Italia dal primo dopoguerra agli anni Settanta*. Milan: Franco Angeli.

Paris, Ivan. 2010a. "Moda e programmazione industriale. Gli influenti nella moda italiana degli anni Sessanta." In *Geografie della moda*, edited by E. Mora, 217–29. Milan: Franco Angeli.

Paris, Ivan. 2010b. "Orígines del Made in Italy. Moda italiana y mercado internazional en la segunda posguerra (1951–1969)." *Revista de Historia Industrial* 42: 121–55.

Paris, Ivan. 2021. "Fashion and Institutions: The AIIA and the Ready-to-Wear Industry in Italy (1945–1975)." *Enterprise & Society* 22 (1): 44–77.

Paulicelli, Eugenia. 2004. *Fashion under Fascism. Beyond the Black Shirt*. Oxford: Berg.

Petri, Rolf. 2006. "Intervento pubblico ed espansione della chimica italiana fino al miracolo economico." In *L'industria chimica italiana nel Novecento*, edited by G. J. Pizzorni, 101–124. Milan: Franco Angeli.

Piccoli, Laura B. 1970. "Incontro con i protagonisti del mondo della moda italiana. Gli industriali dell'abbigliamento." *L'Abbigliamento Italiano* 12 (11) (November): 3.

Pinchera, Valeria. 2009. *La moda in Italia e in Toscana: dalle origini alla globalizzazione*. Venice: Marsilio.

Pinchera, Valeria, and Diego Rinallo. 2020. "The Emergence of Italy as a Fashion Country: Nation Branding and Collective Meaning Creation at Florence's Fashion Shows (1951–1965)." *Business History* 62 (1): 151–78.

Polhemus, Ted. 1994. *Street Style: From Sidewalk to Catwalk*. New York: Thames and Hudson.

Popp, Andrew. 2005. "An Indissoluble Mutual Destiny: The North Staffordshire Potteries and the Limits of Regional Trade Associationalism." *Organization Studies* 26 (12): 1831–49.

Pouillard, Véronique. 2016. "Managing Fashion Creativity: The History of the Chambre Syndicale de la Couture Parisienne During the Interwar Period." *Investigaciones de Historia Económica* 12 (2): 76–89.
Ricciotti, Lazzaro. 1960. "Una *operazione Sud Africa* a cura dell'Ente Italiano della Moda." *L'Abbigliamento Italiano* 2 (4) (April): 3.
Robiola, Elsa. 1967. "Affermazione della moda italiana nel mondo. Islanda." *L'Abbigliamento Italiano* 9 (6) (June): 3.
Robiola, Elsa. 1968. "Trionfo della moda italiana a Dublino." *L'Abbigliamento Italiano* 10 (11) (November): 7.
Robiola, Elsa. 1969. "Esame di coscienza dell'alta moda." *L'Abbigliamento Italiano* 11 (3) (March): 7–8.
Rossetti, Elsa. 1963. "Attività dell'Ente Italiano della Moda. Copenhagen 1963." *L'Abbigliamento Italiano* 5 (July–August): n.p.
Sassatelli, Renata. 2006. "Genere e consumi." In *Il secolo dei consumi. Dinamiche sociali nell'Europa del Novecento*, edited by S. Cavazza and E. Scarpellini, 141–73. Rome: Carocci.
Savage, Jon. 2007. *The Creation of Youth Culture*. New York: Viking.
Scranton, Philip. 1998. "Webs of Productive Association in American Industrialization: Patterns of Institution Formation and Their Limits, Philadelphia, 1880–1930." *Journal of Industrial History* 1 (1): 9–34.
Simonetto, Marzio. 1953. "L'Ente Italiano della Moda ed il pensiero di *Linea*." *Linea. Rivista dell'alta moda*, Spring Edition.
Spadoni, Marcella. 2006. *Il gruppo SNIA dal 1917 al 1951*. Turin: Giappichelli.
Steele, Valerie. 1999. *Paris Fashion: A Cultural History*. Oxford: Berg.
Svendsen, Gunnar Lind Haase. 2014. "Associational Autonomy or Political Influence? The Case of Cooperation Between the Danish Dairies' Buttermark Association and the Danish State, 1900–1912." *Business History* 56 (7): 1084–1110.
Textilia. 1975. "La prima conferenza nazionale della moda." *Textilia* 7 (July): 75–76.
Turra, Alessandra. 2021. "Pitti Uomo: 100 Editions of Men's Fashion." *Women's Wear Daily* 6 (June): 16–17.
Tylecote, Andrew. 2016. "Institutions Matter: but Which Institutions? And How and Why Do They Change?" *Journal of Institutional Economics* 12 (3): 721–42.
Van Rooij, Arjan. 2014. "Sisyphus in Business: Success, Failure and the Different Types of Failure." *Business History* 57 (2): 203–23.
Ville, Simon. 2007. "Rent Seeking or Market Strengthening? Industry Associations in New Zealand Wool Broking." *Business History Review* 81 (2): 297–321.

Walker Laird, Pamela. 2008. "Looking Toward the Future: Expanding Connections for Business Historians." *Enterprise & Society* 9 (4): 575–90.

Yamazaky, Hiroaki, and Matao Miyamoto, eds. 1988. *Trade Associations in Business History: The International Conference on Business History 14*. Proceedings of the Fuji Conference. New York: University of Tokyo Press.

CHAPTER 3

Institutional Failures and Innovation

Abstract The creation of an unstable triangle consisting of the textile industry, the clothing industry, and high fashion was a reflection of a demand structure that in the early 1960s allowed each component to fully exploit its own established and well-defined reference market. Transformations in Italian society disrupted the dualistic framework of the sector and altered the perspective of the many institutional bodies that aimed to represent the interests of individual firms (such as the AIIA, Associazione Italiana Industriali dell'Abbigliamento) or to lead the entire movement (such as the EIM—Ente Italiano della Moda— and the CNMI—Camera Nazionale della Moda Italiana). Throughout the 1970s, many of the main institutions, associations, and organizations that had been involved in protecting and promoting Italian fashion gradually withdrew from the scene. The only body that managed to survive was the CNMI. In this chapter, we will examine the impact the changes described in the preceding chapters had on the institutional framework of Italian fashion and the actors who facilitated the consolidation of the Italian fashion system in international markets during the 1980s.

Keywords Institutional change · Institutional failure · Italian fashion system · Stylist

E. Merlo and I. Paris, *The Italian Fashion System*, Palgrave Studies in Economic History, https://doi.org/10.1007/978-3-031-52375-5_3

3.1 The Result of Twenty Years of Institutional Particularism: the Rise of a New CNMI

This section examines the institutional legacy inherited by the CNMI (National Chamber of Italian Fashion). This subject will be addressed from a dual perspective. Firstly, we will analyse the implications of adopting the institutional model of the *Chambre Syndicale de la Haute Couture*, which was established in France around a century earlier. Subsequently, the consequences related to the role occupied by the CNMI will be highlighted. The CNMI intended to be a 'unifying' organization, but in practice, was the heir of the institutional particularism that characterized Italian fashion in the 1940s and 1950s.

In terms of representation of interests, the emergence of the CNMI was a consequence of the changes described in the preceding chapters and simultaneously represented a rift in the institutional history of the national fashion industry. Similar to the associations born between the 1940s and 1950s, the CNMI aimed to represent and promote Italian fashion. However, unlike other organizations, it pursued this goal through more stringent regulation of the entire sector. For instance, only fashion houses that met specific requirements were allowed to present their collections on various catwalks. A decade earlier, in contrast, an invitation from Giovanni Battista Giorgini was all that was needed to participate in the runway show that marked the birth of Italian fashion in Florence. To bear the title of *casa di alta moda* (high fashion house), a thorough investigation was required, with far from certain outcome, whereas until that point it had been the exclusivity of their clientele (wealthy, elitist, often holding prominent positions in social, political, and cultural circles) that differentiated a fashion house from a mere dressmaker. Access for buyers and journalists to the runway shows was also more tightly regulated, accompanied by the imposition of a code of conduct for the press, which, though regularly broken, established the timing and methods for publishing photographs of the collections shown (press releases).

It can be stated that the birth of the CNMI initiated a process of institutionalization for Italian fashion which was perfectly analogous to events in France around a century earlier, with the establishment of the *Chambre Syndicale de la Haute Couture*. A typewritten document attached to a copy of the Statute of the French association, preserved in the historical archive of CNMI, closely connects the birth of *haute couture* to the creation of the *Chambre*.[1] The document portrayed *haute couture* as revolutionary in terms of the processes of the creation, production, distribution, and consumption of fashion. From the 1980s onwards, literature on the subject considers the emergence of *haute couture* as a pivotal point in fashion history and regard Charles Frédérick Worth as the *couturier* who paved the way for the *haute couture*'s business model. Worth opened his own fashion house in 1857, pioneering innovations in fashion practices and business.[2] Worth further advocated for the creation of the *Chambre Syndicale de la Couture, des Confectionneurs et des Tailleurs pour Dame* (Federation of *Couture*, Clothing Manufacturers, and Tailors for Women) to support and promote individual *couture* houses and Paris *couturier(e)s* as a collective.[3] According to both fashion scholars and professionals, its creation contributed significantly to the establishment and organization of the new Parisian *couture* cluster.[4]

A century after its foundation, could the institutional model of the *Chambre* still be considered relevant and, above all, replicable in the Italian context? Its longevity, as well as the rapidly gained and firmly maintained international reputation of French *haute couture*, had certainly established it as a paradigm that was hard to ignore. Nevertheless, during the same period in which Italy looked to the *Chambre* as a model to protect, represent, and promote the interests of high fashion houses, a process of profound institutional renewal was underway in France. Started in 1954 with the establishment of the *Comité Colbert*, consisting of high-class jewellery firms, gourmet cuisine businesses, the hotel trade, and *haute couture* houses, this process culminated in 1973 with the foundation of the *Fédération Française de la Couture, du Prêt-à-Porter des Couturiers et des Créateurs de Mode* (the French Federation of Fashion, Ready-to-Wear Fashion *Couturier(e)s*, and Fashion Designers). The *Fédération* brought together the *Chambre Syndicale de la haute couture* and the *Chambre Syndicale du Prêt-à-Porter des Couturiers et des Créateurs de Mode*, founded in the same year by Pierre Bergé (co-founder, along with Yves Saint Laurent, of the eponymous fashion house). Over

1 Archivio Storico della camera Nazionale della Moda Italiana (ASCNMI), b. 1, f. 1-1, *Camera sindacale della moda parigina*.

2 De Marly (1980) and Coleman (1989).

3 Palmer (2001, 14).

4 Grumbach (2008) and Pouillard (2016).

the course of two decades, a new institutional structure was thus defined, reflecting two established changes. The first pertained to the extension of the concept of luxury from high fashion to a broader category of goods, which France could capitalize on and enhance the reputation gained from having invented *haute couture* itself. The second pertained to the emergence and success of *prêt-à-porter*, not as a by-product of *haute couture*, but rather as a distinct category in itself which expressed the creativity of a new generation of artist-*couturier(e)s* and mirrored ongoing cultural and social changes. Essentially, the success of *prêt-à-porter* implied the development of a new business model.

In the early 1960s in France, the fashion governance model represented by the *Chambre* was displaying signs of obsolescence. The attempt to emulate it also revealed its incongruity in relation to the Italian context, where, a decade after the official baptism of Italian fashion celebrated by Giorgini in Florence, a chaotic associative pluralism prevailed. Unlike its French counterpart, the CNMI was the latest in a series of associations founded since the late 1940s, not the prototype. The CFMI (Centre of Florence for Italian Fashion), the EIM, the CRAMI (Centre of Rome for Italian High Fashion), the CIAC (International Center for the Arts and Costume) of Venice, and the *Centro Mediterraneo della Moda e dell'Artigianato* (Mediterranean Center of Fashion and Handicrafts) of Naples became members, but the CNMI did not embody a federal institutional model similar to that which was forming in France. The associations that joined had the same institutional status as all other categories of members, including the textile, clothing, and accessory industries, chambers of commerce, and, naturally, fashion houses. While taking the *Chambre* as a model, the CNMI had not fully embraced its monocratic institutional model, as all pre-existing associations that joined maintained their independence.

The institutional model that emerged with the birth of the CNMI was an expression of a historical legacy that reflected not only the existence of a plurality of associations but also the way in which they interacted. The relationship established between these associations and the CNMI replicated on a larger scale that which had already occurred in the previous decade between the CFMI, the EIM, and the CRAMI and persisted into the 1970s. This was a connection that, while pursuing goals of dialogue and coordination, had actually translated into cross-control by placing the same individuals, who were often politically influential, in their respective leadership bodies. This was the case, for example, for Dino Alfieri and

Amos Ciabattoni. A staunch supporter of the fascist regime, Alfieri had served as a deputy, ambassador, and, between 1936 and 1939, Minister of Popular Culture, a position that had led him to take an interest in the fashion sector and represent the government in the *Ente Nazionale della Moda* (National Body of Fashion). Still highly active in the post-World War II republican political scene, Alfieri held positions in the leadership bodies of the EIM (Italian Fashion Body) and the CFMI while he was also President of the CIM (Italian Fashion Centre) in Milan and MITAM. Amos Ciabattoni, who was national leader of the most important political party of the time (Christian Democrats), began to be involved in the fashion industry, mandated by another influential party colleague, Emilio Colombo, who was appointed Minister of Industry in 1959. In his role as secretary of the CRAMI, Ciabattoni helped in the establishment of the CNMI, of which he was the general secretary for a decade before becoming President of the EIM in 1976.

The institutional legacy inherited by the CNMI was clearly evident in the goals of dialogue and coordination that were the basis of the initiative which was initiated by the CRAMI in late 1960. On that occasion, representatives of some renowned high fashion houses had gathered in Rome to discuss the schedule of shows to be organized in January of the following year. The meeting had been hastily arranged after Paris decided to bring the dates of its own shows forward. The rescheduling of the French calendar caused clashes with the Italian schedule and jeopardized the organization of the Florence and Rome catwalk shows. The Parisian decision thus prompted the CRAMI to address the delicate issue of calendar coordination. An agreement was proposed to the CFMI, which seized the opportunity to enhance the proposal by suggesting a broader collaboration through the creation of a national entity, modelled on that already working in France.[5]

However, the proposal fell on deaf ears. It was Amos Ciabattoni himself, in his capacity as the general secretary of the CRAMI, who explained the reasons behind it. The proposal put forth by the CFMI "lacked a unified spirit [...] and did not respect priority rules".[6] The Florentine proposal, much more ambitious than that from Rome, suffered

[5] ASCNMI, b.1, f. 1-3, *Centro Alta Moda Italiana - Roma, Riunione di alcune ditte interessate all'alta moda.*

[6] ASCNMI, b. 107, f. 107-1, *Convegno Positano*, 5 September 1961.

from both arrogance and naivety. On the one hand, in a highly competitive and fragmented institutional context such as Italy, it placed the CFMI and the CRAMI, as well as the different types of fashion showcased on their respective catwalks, on the same level. On the other hand, it failed to take into account the foreseeable adverse reaction of the EIM, which, as the sole legally recognized entity, would undoubtedly have asserted its right to exclusively represent Italian fashion.[7]

However, it was Ciabattoni himself who revived the idea shortly thereafter. In a letter sent in 1962 to the presidents of the CIM (Dino Alfieri), the CFMI (Giovanni Giorgini), and the EIM (Vladimiro Rossini), the General Secretary of the CRAMI reassured his colleagues of the genuine intentions of the new organization.[8] Despite being quite similar to the French *Chambre*, the CNMI would not limit the autonomy of the existing bodies. Nonetheless, the success of the initiative was far from certain. This was confirmed by Ciabattoni himself in a confidential letter sent only to Giorgini. Ciabattoni reiterated the relevance of the French model ("Is there a French trade union chamber? Yes! So why shouldn't the National Chamber of Italian Fashion be created with the same characteristics and the same purposes?"), but he did not hide his concerns about the challenges its implementation would face in an Italian context.[9] The initiative would certainly have encountered hostility from a public entity like the EIM, which believed it could (and should) "meddle in everything and everywhere". However, according to Ciabattoni, this risk would have decreased if the CNMI had been administered by representatives of the professional categories rather than by entities or centres.[10] To encourage the CFMI's participation in the project, Ciabattoni emphasized its centrality as an entity which was concerned with high fashion, much like the CRAMI. On the contrary, the involvement of EIM could be dispensed with, as it was closer to the interests of the ready-to-wear industry.

[7] ASCNMI, b. 1, f. 1-5, *Centro Romano Alta Moda Italiana - Roma, Appunto riservato del 3 maggio 1962.*

[8] ASCNMI, b. 1, f. 1- 7, Letter from Amos Ciabattoni to Giovanni Giorgini, Dino Alfieri, and Vladimiro Rossini, 12 May 1962.

[9] ASCNMI, b. 16, f. 16-4, Letter from Amos Ciabattoni to Giovanni Giorgini, 11 May 1962.

[10] Idem.

The pursuit of balance among the diverse and sometimes conflicting interests represented by the CFMI, the CRAMI, and the EIM was a constant part of the CNMI's activities. This institutional innovation, characterized by the increased significance of representatives from professional categories in the governing bodies—a development that garnered attention only in the case of notable defections—was overshadowed.[11] The governing bodies themselves responded slowly to ongoing economic, social, and cultural changes, underestimating their impact, especially in terms of their effects on matters of particular concern to fashion houses, such as the scheduling of the calendar and the organization of catwalk shows. It is not surprising, therefore, that by the end of the 1960s, the CNMI acknowledged the existence of the first Milanese initiatives (referred to as "fragmentary") without considering them an obstacle to the CNMI's project, which envisioned four distinct events: presentations of high fashion collections, which would continue to take place in Rome in January and July, and presentations of knitwear and prêt-à-porter collections scheduled for April and October in Florence. The 1970s, as we will see, would nevertheless force the CNMI to swiftly change its strategies.

3.2 Institutional Anachronism

The shift in demand structure seen in the second half of the 1960s incentivized stakeholders within the Italian fashion industry, including the institutions tasked with representing its interests, to collaborate more. This approach envisioned long-term benefits but also entailed immediate costs that were not always distributed evenly among the parties involved. The situation that emerged risked causing a definitive split between the first tier (high fashion) and the third tier (ready-to-wear) of Italian fashion, greatly benefiting foreign competition (particularly French *prêt-à-porter*). In this section, we will analyse the main relational dynamics between different fashion institutions and their effects on the structure of the Italian fashion system.

The 1960s marked the beginning of a new phase for the Italian fashion industry. The protagonists of this transformation were women and the younger generations, who were increasingly active in expressing their

[11] ASCNMI, b. 4, f. 4-1, *Comunicato stampa*, 4 April 1962.

clothing preferences. The ready-to-wear industry and high fashion recognized the signs of this change and responded accordingly. The former sought to improve production quality, while the latter promoted an intermediate range of products capable of combining the exclusivity of high fashion with the potential of mass production. The gradual reconstruction of the European economy and the process of forming the European Common Market offered greater opportunities but also increased competition. This stimulated new policies aimed at improving the organization of the entire production chain, from the creative phase to promotional activities.

In the preceding chapters, we described some of the early experiences of collaboration which, even if some initiatives were individual in nature, saw vertical and horizontal integration as the path to consolidating the success of the Italian fashion industry. Certainly, one could not yet speak of a true 'system', but the gradual shift of focus to the new needs of the consumer changed the perspective of all involved. Despite various experiments, an intermediate production level capable of combining the value of a *griffe* representing a well-defined and identifiable style with a competitive retail price was still lacking in Italy.

The situation was different from that of France, where multiple levels of *prêt-à-porter* offered consumers a variety of options. At the top of the list were the most expensive items of the so-called *prêt-à-porter de luxe* (or *création*), produced by a few famous *haute couture* houses and marketed at a price ranging from 30 to 80 USD (this exclusive club included names such as Pierre Cardin, Yves Saint Laurent, Jean Dessés, and Guy Laroche). At the bottom were the *prêt-à-porter Riviera* (or *Côte d'Azur*) models, produced by around twenty companies and sold for prices between 6 and 60 USD.[12] In addition to the variety of garments on sale, the prices of French garments were generally lower than their Italian equivalents.[13] It mattered little if the overall quality was not always the best. An example of this is the case of Saint Laurent, one of the world's most famous fashion houses in the field of ready-made fashion. When the French *couturier* opened a new store in Milan in 1967, the city was mesmerized, despite all kinds of clothing already being readily available and despite the fact that the overall quality of the offered garments was considered to be inferior

[12] Robiola (1967).

[13] Amica (1965).

to that of the finest Italian industrially produced garments. The success of Saint Laurent was certainly linked to competitive pricing, but what mattered most was its "prestigious and fascinating" label.[14] The designer label represented a kind of seal—guaranteeing the spirit and personality of the designer himself, a pattern born from creativity rather than the anonymity that still characterized much of the Italian-produced ready-to-wear clothing.

It is important to highlight how the fashion press intentionally used the terms 'designer' and 'pattern' rather than 'creator' and 'dress'. The designers of French *prêt-à-porter* were already engaging on a daily basis with the demands of industrial production and knew how to blend the creative phase with production and distribution, in order to offer models suitable for a new category of consumers.[15] In France, the relationship between creation and industry had already undergone a radical change, which had improved and cemented the position of French *prêt-à-porter* in international markets. This was confirmed by the presence of representatives from major New York department stores at the Paris ready-to-wear week as early as the start of the 1960s. Therefore, it should come as no surprise that significant names such as Jean Dessès, for instance, had decided to permanently transition to *prêt-à-porter*.[16]

The French industries had also attempted to integrate the creative phase within their operations. In the first half of the 1960s, names such as Emmanuelle Khanh, Christiane Bailly, Michèle Rosier, and Gérard Pipard collaborated with ready-to-wear companies.[17] Despite attempting to follow in its footsteps, the sporadic partnerships between Italian *couturier(e)s* and the ready-to-wear industry had not achieved the same results. The so-called *alta moda pronta* (high fashion ready-to-wear), which used the French *prêt-à-porter de luxe* as its model and found its ideal home on the catwalks of Florence, failed to achieve the same results.

Replicating in Italy what was happening in France required modification of the entire production cycle.[18] The industry had to plan production at least one year in advance, and this explains why, with the lack of

[14] Bruno (1967).

[15] Lipovetsky (1987, 131–53).

[16] L'Abbigliamento Italiano (AI) (1963a).

[17] AI (1963b) and Mossetti (1967).

[18] Ronco (1971).

the creative phase, the activity of forecasting and supporting new trends became increasingly important. As we saw in the previous chapter, the path initially pursued and supported by industry associations was to rely on *ad hoc* fashion councils. The weak link in the entire planning process, and a source of greater concern, was the inherent difficulty in fairly distributing risks and benefits among all parties involved. This situation had already emerged regarding the individual agreements described earlier. Nevertheless, this type of approach was also adopted at an institutional level, both among industry organizations and between these organizations and individual businesses, always under the supervision of the relevant national institutions (starting with those established by the ministries most involved).

As a representative of high fashion houses, the CNMI quickly became active in building a network of relationships with other stakeholders in the fashion supply chain, starting from the textile and ready-to-wear companies. Special attention was also given to relationships with the media (especially the specialized press) and an open communication channel with the political system was maintained. In the former case, the goal was to construct a narrative conducive to the success of Italian fashion, particularly high fashion. The CNMI's ambition was to become a hub for the convergence and dissemination of news regarding the whole sector.[19] In the second case, the goal was to exert pressure at parliamentary and governmental levels to gain greater attention for what was a strategic sector for the national economy. However, the ultimate aim was to promote the centrality of the CNMI to this process, starting with the request for the necessary funding.[20] From the very beginning, the CNMI cultivated relationships with the business world, not solely to raise the necessary finance for it to function. The lack of resources was also a serious concern for the affiliated fashion houses, which required capital to organize production and promote it both in Italy and abroad. Through the establishment of an effective textile-read to wear-high fashion triangle, the CNMI aimed to strengthen the entire sector, thereby encouraging governmental bodies to define and implement an effective 'fashion policy'. The cornerstone of the entire project

[19] ASCNMI, b. 3, *Relazione del Consiglio Direttivo all'Assemblea Generale dei soci del 16 Dicembre 1966*.

[20] E.g. see the numerous letters from Amos Ciabattoni to the members of the Italian Parliament and Government in ASCNMI, b. 4.

naturally remained high fashion, which was still considered "a propulsive and prestigious force of considerable importance" by all parties.[21]

Conversely, political institutions also had a vested interest in maintaining control over a rapidly expanding sector with enormous potential, especially within the context of the European Common Market. The two committees established within the Ministries of Industry and Foreign Trade confirmed the interest of government institutions. The goal was to oversee and guide the system, while playing a mediating role in agreements between high fashion houses and individual industries. The *Comitato Consultivo Permanente* (Permanent Advisory Committee) of the Ministry of Foreign Trade was established in July 1963 during a conference organized by representatives of high fashion, the textile and ready-to-wear industries to initiate collaborative agreements. In March 1964, the Committee approved a sectoral agreement between the textile industry and high fashion that pursued this objective. By establishing closer collaboration aimed at directing their respective production, the agreement aimed to enhance the quality of the former and empower the latter through the exclusive supply of quality fabrics, providing funding in exchange for advertising, and implementing joint promotional programmes in Italy and abroad. The magazine *I Tessili Nuovi* would become the official organ of the agreement, and a dedicated office was envisioned to facilitate the programme (*Centro per lo Sviluppo e l'Esportazione dei Prodotti Tessili, dell'Abbigliamento e della Moda*, Centre for the Development and Export of Textile, Clothing, and Fashion Products).[22] Therefore, awareness of the necessity to collaborate in order to consolidate and develop the entire fashion sector was becoming evident. The agreement, not only desired but also supervised by governmental institutions, represented a significant achievement from an economic perspective (essential for fashion houses) and from an advertising standpoint (crucial for the textile industries). However, in a broader perspective, its aim was to provide a foundation for strong and lasting relations

[21] ASCNMI, b. 3, *Relazione del Consiglio Direttivo all'Assemblea Generale dei soci del 29 Ottobre 1964*.

[22] ASCNMI, b. 3, *Relazione del Consiglio Direttivo all'Assemblea Generale dei soci del 29 Ottobre 1964* and *Relazione del Consiglio Direttivo all'Assemblea Generale dei soci del 16 Dicembre 1967*.

between individual operators from both sectors and among representatives of their respective industry associations, fostering synergies to the benefit of the entire Italian fashion system.

The CNMI also promoted collaboration by entering into agreements with individual companies. An example of this is the agreement signed in 1964 with Rhodiatoce, a Lombardy-based company that produced man-made fibres such as nylon, terital, and rhodia. The businesses with substantial immediately available funds were primarily textile companies, and Rhodiatoce had already opened an account with 15 million ITL with the CNMI, which was in financial difficulty, in 1963.[23] It was a true collaboration agreement that guaranteed the CNMI a non-repayable contribution of 50 million ITL in total for the first year alone. In exchange for this funding, Rhodiatoce demanded the establishment of a collaborative relationship with the fashion houses which were part of the CNMI, placing the Lombardy company in a privileged position.

By signing the agreement, Rhodiatoce demonstrated that it had effectively implemented a part of the arrangements reached at a ministerial level. The agreement was extended until 1969 and then not further renewed by Rhodiatoce itself. This was followed by those with Snia Viscosa (from 1969) and Lanerossi (from 1970), which also provided for the inclusion of trusted persons in the governing bodies of the CNMI.[24] The case of Lanerossi, part of the ENI Group (a multinational corporation established by the Italian state in 1953), is of particular interest. The agreement with Lanerossi included a significant innovation: the establishment within the CNMI itself of a *Comitato Alta moda-Industria* (High Fashion-Industry Committee) composed of Lanerossi, Snia Viscosa, and several high fashion houses. The aim of the Committee was to annually define fashion trends that all CNMI-affiliated fashion houses would need to adhere to, in exchange for a financial contribution proportionate to their compliance with said trends. Following this agreement, the influence of the industry on the CNMI's activities increased significantly, which also had repercussions on individual fashion houses. In exchange for funding, these fashion houses would see their creative freedom limited in part, sacrificed to accommodate the needs of the industry.

[23] ACNMI, b. 51, f. 51-8, *Verbale del Consiglio Direttivo del 18 Aprile 1964.*

[24] ASCNMI, b. 55, f. 55-2, *Ratifica accordo di collaborazione Snia Viscosa – Camera Nazionale*; ASCNMI, b. 56, f. 56-3, *Accordo Camera Nazionale – Lanerossi.*

With regard to the relationship between high fashion and the ready-to-wear industry, it was the EIM rather than the CNMI that pursued collective initiatives. In October 1962, the first national meeting titled *Moda e Industria dell'Abbigliamento* (Fashion and Clothing Industry) was held in Turin. This event was promoted by the EIM at the request of those operating in the sector to explore the possibility of coordinating their respective production policies, with a particular focus on the creation of patterns. The occasion was an opportunity to push for an increase in the quality of ready-to-wear garments and to provide high fashion with new opportunities for expansion into more competitive and profitable production.[25]

The preconditions were favourable because both parties had a strong focus on collaboration. Already in January 1962, some companies interested in establishing contacts with high fashion had been invited to the Florentine fashion shows held at *Palazzo Pitti*. The aforementioned meeting in Turin was also useful for promoting the CNMI as a new body which was institutionally representative of high fashion. This proved the will to go beyond individual initiatives to develop broader and more cohesive collaborations between high fashion and ready-to-wear in order to develop an intermediate level of production.[26] However, a clear contradiction remained in the background, the symptom of an outdated view of the fashion industry. One of the goals of the meeting in Turin, in fact, was still to define and emphasize a clear distinction between "fashion house" and "garment industry".[27]

The issue of coordination at a 'sectoral' level was reiterated within the *Comitato Consultivo della Moda* (Advisory Committee for Fashion), established in 1967 at the Ministry of Industry under the leadership of Giulio Andreotti. The same point was raised by the Minister for Foreign Trade through the aforementioned *Comitato Consultivo Permanente*. Prompted by its two main shareholders, the EIM established a dedicated study commission in February 1969 (the *Commissione EIM*). The goal was to focus on collaboration between the creative sector and the industrial production sector.

[25] Ministero dell'Industria, del Commercio e dell'Artigianato (1969, 107).

[26] ASCNMI, b. 3, *Relazione del Consiglio Direttivo all'Assemblea Generale dei soci del 16 Dicembre 1967*, p. 37.

[27] Ministero dell'Industria, del Commercio e dell'Artigianato (1969, 117–18).

The EIM Commission was made up of five representatives of the ready-to-wear industry (GFT, Hettemarks, Marzotto, Max Mara, and UniMac) and five high fashion houses (Galitzine, Gregoriana, Mila Schön, Sarli, and Veneziani).[28] The work of the Commission was based on a shared vision of the need for greater collaboration. Defining the technical details and operational proposals, however, proved to be more complex, therefore it initially focused on a trial period limited to reaching an agreement on colours only. The pursuit of the means and tools required to implement the initiative was a significant matter, starting with the acquisition of sufficient financial resources to reach the main objectives. The idea was to request funding from the two ministries involved, ensuring a foundation of economic support for participating fashion houses. The ministerial capital would then be supplemented by a fund established and managed by the participating companies (40 million ITL for each of the initially planned two years), which would independently determine how much would be given to those fashion houses deemed most suitable. The advertising activities undertaken by individual companies using their own resources would further contribute to sustain the trends promoted by the fashion houses which were involved in the project.

Without delving too deeply into the technical details of agreements that were at risk of being too rigid for an industry that needed greater flexibility, an approach which was still high fashion oriented emerges in this case, with the fashion houses at the centre of the system due to the steadfast belief in their role as the sole trendsetters. However, reality showed that high fashion was becoming less and less of a leader in terms of establishing trends. These types of agreements therefore reflected the anachronism of the Italian fashion institutions of the time in relation to an industry undergoing significant transformation, also in terms of its major influencers.

Undoubtedly the failure of these initiatives was also linked to more specific and no less relevant reasons. According to Jole Veneziani, for example, collective agreements between high fashion and the ready-to-wear industry failed due to purely economic reasons (which, from her perspective, disadvantaged high fashion in particular). In an interview given in 1969, Veneziani also highlighted the reluctance of *couturier(e)s*

[28] ASCNMI, b. 55, f. 55-5, *Verbale del Consiglio Direttivo del 12 Dicembre 1969*.

to share their own brand with the industry, as it was considered the exclusive result of their work. On the contrary, Biki emphasized the inability of many fashion designers to provide the industry with designs which were not only stylistically appreciable, but also technically valid and could be reproduced on a large scale. Essentially, these *couturier(e)s* lacked the ability to manage a production cycle inherently different from that of a high fashion house, which saw the design of the model as just one of several aspects to consider.[29] However, the approach that had become detached from the reality of the main fashion institutions and most of their associates remained the primary reason for not only the failure of various collaborative initiatives, but also for the broader project of 'centralized planning of fashion', which was also supported by the government institutions most involved.

It was precisely within this context that some of the smaller and more dynamic enterprises began to wonder whether fashion and centralized planning could really coexist. After all, it was a process marked by a high degree of approximation and, moreover, carried out in a context of extreme variability. It was necessary to evaluate, in a typical creative industry in which managing creativity and business is a complex process, the hidden costs in terms of competitiveness of the planning efforts made by fashion institutions.[30] High fashion (not only in Italy) was facing a challenging situation, to the advantage of the so-called ready-made fashion. As early as the mid-1960s, authoritative observers wondered "how much high fashion was still in fashion".[31] Also for the CNMI, the need to expand into an industrial dimension had become "clear and pressing". In the second half of the 1960s, CNMI members had been repeatedly urged to broaden their scope, encompassing not only the primary activity of high fashion but also areas such as *prêt-à-porter*, boutiques, and even ready-to-wear itself. The conviction that achieving this goal would be challenging without the contribution of the industry and its corresponding production structure was strong. However, at the heart of the project, high fashion remained the pivotal actor.[32]

[29] Capalbi (1966), Piccoli (1969a, 1969b).

[30] On this topic see Pouillard (2016).

[31] Capalbi (1966).

[32] ASCNMI, b. 3, *Relazione del Consiglio direttivo dell'Assemblea generale dei soci del 16 Dicembre 1967*, p. 37.

In addition to this, there was a need to bring order to the taxonomy of the intermediate production segment which was between high fashion and ready-to-wear; this segment encompassed certain types of production still in search of their own identity.[33] According to the CNMI, the distinction between *prêt-à-porter di alta moda* (high fashion *prêt-à-porter*) and *alta moda pronta* was extremely subtle and so arbitrary that it rendered them essentially interchangeable. In both cases, they were small-to-medium-scale industrial productions, but to qualify as *alta moda pronta*, a garment also had to meet the requirement of originality. According to the CNMI, it was this aspect that differentiated "creation" from mere "production".[34] Yet how could one ascertain the presence or absence of such a requirement? This was an even more challenging task in a context where the clear distinction that had existed until then between high fashion, boutique fashion, and *prêt-à-porter* was fading. The boundary lines often blurred, overlapping and crossing to give rise to intermediate production categories that even industry professionals struggled to differentiate, but which in practice neither the high fashion houses nor the major Italian ready-to-wear industries managed to fully occupy.

The fundamental error was to deem it impossible for the industry to develop within itself that creative phase necessary to establish a foothold in the market, even though the concept of fashion generated by new socio-cultural phenomena was well suited to the needs of mass production, with models which needed less intricate workmanship, less artisanal finishing, and shorter production times.[35] The misconception still lay in regarding high fashion as the cornerstone of the system, under the belief that without the *couturier(e)*, the main "source of inspiration" for most clothing industries would be lost.[36] Even the mini skirt launched by Mary Quant was considered the little sister of certain high fashion designs by Courrèges or Ungaro.[37] However, it was forgotten that the global success of these clothing items had been achieved solely through mass market

[33] Robiola (1968).

[34] ASCNMI, b. 3, f. 3-1, *Regolamento per la qualificazione e la classificazione delle attività della moda del 1974* (artt. 9-12).

[35] Messina (1987, 28).

[36] Capalbi (1962).

[37] Robiola (1971).

production, aimed at a market segment far removed from that of the fashion houses.

Moreover, many Italian fashion houses also struggled with economic difficulties stemming from high production costs that were not offset by adequate revenues. This was compounded by the burden of producing frequent collections. The now six-monthly renewal necessitated constant change, with a significant impact not only in economic terms. The need to design new collections at an increasing pace forced *couturier(e)s* to "burn themselves on the catwalk", thereby compromising their ability to maintain a guiding role in setting trends.[38]

The French *prêt-à-porter*, therefore, served as a model to be followed by Italian fashion houses as well. Before associating his name with a major Tuscan clothing company, Emilio Schuberth stated: "All women have the right to dress well, even those who cannot spend much".[39] However, even in this seemingly forward-thinking stance concealed the usual anachronistic approach of Italian high fashion. The attempt to link the *couturier(e)*'s name to industrial products, in fact, aimed to prevent the ready-to-wear industries themselves from entering the intermediate market segment. This explains why the Florentine experience of *alta moda pronta* was in contrast to the *confezione di lusso* (luxury ready-to-wear) initiative developed from 1969 at the SAMIA stands in Turin (*Modaselezione*).[40]

However, both initiatives failed to achieve the desired outcomes. For *alta moda pronta*, early attempts at collaboration failed largely because high fashion tailors were unable to manage the numerous variables of a complex production process. They had little knowledge of the dynamics of either the industry or the commercial marketplace. This translated into an inability to combine the qualitative characteristics of high fashion with a new pricing policy and mass market standards of wearability. Furthermore, the choice of Florence as a platform for the launch of *alta moda pronta* proved to be a mistake. The formality of shows based on the high fashion model was poorly adapted to a type of production aimed at a young and dynamic market segment. Given this challenge to the status of

[38] Ricca (1968) and Robiola (1969, 1970).

[39] Cecchi (1968).

[40] On the reasons why many high fashion houses concentrated on *alta moda pronta*, see ASCNMI, b. 161, f. 161-7, *Relazione Consiglio direttivo Camera*. For developments in *confezione di lusso*, see the numerous reports included in *L'Abbigliamento Italiano*.

the Florence catwalk, many high fashion houses moved the presentation of their collections to Milan. At least three related causes account for the failure of *confezione di lusso*. First, it was unable to establish leadership in the definition of taste. Second, its production practices lacked the flexibility that would be essential to meet the notably polymorphous fashion trends of the middle of the decade. Third, while production tended to diversify as little as possible, the burgeoning youth market was seeking to express a specific identity via its choice of clothing. The industry simply lacked the ability to respond effectively to contemporary socio-economic changes.[41]

Despite the broader context and the challenges encountered, at the end of the 1960s the lack of coordination between high fashion and ready-to-wear was still an issue addressed at the institutional level. The aforementioned *Commissione EIM* was established in 1969 also to address the delicate topic of the use of the *couturier(e)*'s name by industry.[42] This was a central issue, which even the *Comitato Consultivo della Moda* viewed as difficult to implement due to the lack of credible partners.[43] As a result, the debate shifted towards the usual economic and financial issues, particularly focusing on who should provide the necessary resources to implement (still and only) the coordination of colour. The CNMI itself, which had engaged in the arrangement primarily because of its economically favourable aspects, had definitively confirmed its end by 1969. Therefore, the institutional coordination of high fashion and industry remained a chimera.

Although it had become evident that establishing a second tier of fashion in Italy through collaboration between high fashion and the large textile and clothing industries was impossible, professionals had not yet given up hope. Despite prominent figures such as Biki not believing that an action like that implemented with GFT could be organically extended to the entire world of high fashion and industry, the theme of coordination and agreements was not abandoned. Jole Veneziani, for example, declared herself "completely in agreement" with the need for collaboration. Guido Matura of GFT saw coordination as "the only path". Giulio

[41] Paris (2010, 538–39).

[42] ASCNMI, b. 55, f. 55-5, *Lavori e documenti della commissione di studio per il coordinamento tra l'alta moda e l'industria della confezione*; ASCNMI, b. 55, c. 55-5, *Accordo "alta moda-confezione": valutazioni e orientamenti per l'approvazione dell'assemblea.*

[43] Ministero dell'Industria, del Commercio e dell'Artigianato (1969, 108).

Goehring of the AIIA (Italian Clothing Industry Association) recalled how an improvement to the image of industrial production was the necessary prerequisite for any possible increase in both domestic demand and exports. The Christian Democrat Vittorino Colombo, former Minister of Foreign Trade, was of the same mind. Biki's thoughts, therefore, stood in opposition to those of important figures in high fashion, industry, and institutions who identified the lack of coordination as the main cause of the challenging situation in both high fashion and the well-established clothing industries. The fact that this situation was bordering on paroxysmal was confirmed not only by the excessive proliferation of organizations, associations, and committees all claiming some form of coordinating role, but also by the need to "coordinate the coordinators themselves"—the tragicomic outcome of a debate that marked the challenging state of affairs at the time.[44]

By the late 1960s, therefore, there were three paths that high fashion had pursued to enter the ready-made fashion production. The first one had been that of boutique fashion, but this involved almost entirely artisan production which did not necessarily involve a close relationship with industry. The second one, although yielding commercial results which were below expectations and far from the French successes, was that of *alta moda pronta*, a solution where models were mass-produced by external workshops. This was a semi-artisanal process that, while retaining some characteristics of high fashion, employed specific measures to streamline the production process (such as partial use of machines and simplification of designs to reduce fabric usage) and lowered production costs. Finally, the third path was to hand over specific patterns which were tailored for large-scale production to industry and then sell them under the label of the fashion house. However, these collaborations did not yield the expected results, as they remained sporadic and limited initiatives, often experimental in nature and without long-term agreements.[45]

In October 1970, institutional contacts resumed when the EIM and the CNMI decided to re-examine previous agreements. In particular, it was once again Amos Ciabattoni who identified the possibility of reaching an agreement only through a broadly representative political instrument, rather than through technical collaboration. However, this agreement also

[44] Piccoli (1969b, 1969c), AI (1969), and Informazioni EIM (1969).

[45] Informazioni EIM (1970).

had exclusively economic and financial contents. Nevertheless, governmental institutions once again expressed their full support. Antonio Gava, a significant figure in Italy's primary political party, saw this renewed agreement as a guiding tool for the entire national fashion sector.[46] The reaction of the press was quite favourable as well—perhaps because the frustration that had built up over a decade of failed attempts and the impending crisis had made any potential step forward an unexpected result. According to Elisa Massai of the *Corriere della Sera*, one of the leading Italian newspapers, the social and economic significance of the fashion production chain was such that nothing could be left "to chance or whim" of its two main protagonists (high fashion and the large-scale clothing industry).[47] However, these statements did not take into consideration the growing significance of the intermediate level of production which had no intention of participating in the initiative (and which no longer had the AIIA as its reference association), in the same way as prominent supporters of the CNMI such as Biki, Germana Marucelli, the Sorelle Fontana, and Emilio Pucci.[48]

With these premises, the High Fashion and Ready-to-wear Industry Arrangement (*Accordo Alta Moda-Industria*) was signed in 1971 by the EIM, the CNMI, the AIIA, and the union representatives of the textile industry and producers of artificial and synthetic fibres. The goal remained the same: to attempt to connect the creative world with that of industry and initiate the development of a second tier of fashion in Italy. In essence, the agreement did not deviate from its predecessors and thus represented the unsuccessful outcome of a period that had attempted to revitalize the prospects of high fashion and the large ready-to-wear industry through a strategy of planning.[49] Through this agreement, there was a mistaken belief that the market could be reassured by standardizing demand, with the aim of achieving four objectives: industrial production of garments in line with high fashion designs, prolonging the lifespan of a fashion idea, simplifying production planning, and offering better protection to stores against the risk of unsold stock. This was, once again, an agreement

[46] Piccoli (1969d) and Zincone (1971).

[47] Massai (1971).

[48] Calandri (1971).

[49] The complete text of the agreement and the main comments of the press are detailed in Informazioni EIM (1971).

imposed from the top and as such could not be seen as the beginning of a new phase. However, the High Fashion Ready-to-wear Industry Arrangement marked the end of the aspiration of high fashion houses and large-scale ready-to-wear manufacturers to successfully cover the wide intermediate market sector consisting of consumers who were no longer solely interested in a good quality-price ratio.

The first (and also last) *Conferenza Nazionale della Moda* (National Meeting on Fashion), strongly advocated for in 1975 by Amos Ciabattoni (who by then had become involved with the management of EIM), was the final swan song.[50] There was a substantial disconnect from the reality that was profoundly different from that of the 1950s and early 1960s, which had contributed to the launch of Italian fashion and its early successes in international markets. The analysis of the context carried out during the meeting in Turin was valuable, but the solutions offered were inadequate, effectively overtaken by the actions of a new generation of businesses and designers who, now centred in Milan, had initiated a new period for Italian fashion—the era of the so-called stylism. The *Conferenza Nazionale della Moda* represented a turning point and marked the beginning of a phase which saw the re-evaluation of high fashion and the renewal of industry. This process led to the permanent closure of important businesses that had made history in Italian ready-to-wear in the preceding decades (such as Rosier, Hettemarks, and UniMac). This ended an era during which attempts had been made, through general and organic agreements, to establish in Italy the second level of fashion, but without achieving a 'functional connection' between high fashion and industry. Instead, the process had to be based on rethinking the creation phase based on industrial needs and on the reorganization of the industrial planning considering the requirements of fashion designers.[51] It is difficult to say whether this was primarily due to the lack of willingness on the part of many *couturier(e)s* and industrialists or to the impossibility, perhaps due to incapacity, of adapting to each other's needs. However, while the first and third levels of Italian fashion were going through a period of increasing difficulties and transformations, gradually, entities emerged that were no longer solely concerned with containing and domesticating external stimuli but were willing to invest in rethinking the

[50] Ente Italiano della Moda (1976).

[51] Merlo (2003, 99).

organization of their own production and redefining their own style and image.

3.3 The Unexpected Winner: The Stylist as Institutional Innovation

This section focuses on the institutional changes which fostered the emergence of Milan as an international fashion hub during the 1970s. In those years, industrial entrepreneurs and promising designers signed licensing agreements that paved the way for a new model of governance to emerge, based on the fashion designer (the so-called *stylist*) as the key institutional actor who defined the rules of the new Italian fashion system.

During the 1970s, the pressures for change which were the result of the economic and social context highlighted the inertia of the main institutions of Italian fashion. In particular, the CNMI gradually lost its central role in lobbying and managing relations with other associations and businesses.

From the middle of the decade onwards, a series of events marked the beginning of a new path not only for the CNMI but for the entire Italian fashion industry. In this context, the growing prominence of the city of Milan would redefine the geography of Italian fashion. 1975, in particular, is considered a turning point. *Assomoda*, the association that brought together agents and representatives in the clothing sector, had been running a new event called *Milanovendemoda* in Milan since 1969. Although initially overlooked by the CNMI itself, the new Milanese event had, from its early editions, captured the attention of the public and international buyers, standing out in the Italian Fashion Show landscape as a modern launchpad for knitwear, high-fashion boutiques, and ready-to-wear, or that intermediate level of production long sought after and appreciated by the public. It was indeed in 1975 that the CNMI fully recognized the importance acquired by Milan, promoting and supporting its members who intended to participate in the Milanese event.[52] This decision unilaterally ended the dispute fuelled by the CFMI and which had been ongoing since 1971 when the board of directors of the CNMI decided to establish a new sector called *alta moda pronta*. The CFMI's

[52] ASCNMI, b. 16, f. 16-6, Letter from Luciano Radi to Franco Tancredi, 18 September 1975.

immediate reaction was one of opposition. President Franco Tancredi considered the new sector to be a duplicate of the existing *prêt-à-porter di alta moda*, which revolved around the Florence fashion shows. According to the then-President of the CNMI, former deputy and future Minister for Relations with Parliament, Luciano Radi, the CNMI's choice to support its members' participation in Milanese fashion events was nothing more than a product of simple realism. Every attempt to provide the CFMI with the means to absorb what was eloquently termed the "Milanese secession", which was initially underestimated but over time emerged as a potential threat even to the institutional stability of Italian fashion, had proven to be futile.[53] Milan was establishing itself as a new frontier, and the CNMI could only acknowledge the fact and look in that direction.

The establishment of the new *alta moda pronta* sector, occurring during a period of serious difficulty for the CFMI and the decline of the Florence fashion shows as the main stage for Italian fashion, appeared to be a hostile move. On the one hand, it signalled the deterioration of the relationship between the CNMI and the CFMI, but more broadly, it foreshadowed the breakdown of the institutional framework constructed over the previous two decades. The same fate befell the CRAMI. The logo and name continued to appear on fashion event calendars in Rome, but the ties with the CNMI gradually loosened, becoming almost occasional—and in some cases even contentious—during the 1980s.[54]

In 1976, a special supplement of the prestigious *Women's Wear Daily*, published on the 25th anniversary of the first Italian Fashion Show in Florence, highlighted the new role of Milan. The supplement began with a tribute to Giovanni Giorgini and showcased creations from the most prominent names in Italian fashion, with a particular focus on those labels that had contributed most to the conquest of international markets (especially in the United States). However, the advertising messages accompanying the booklet, which inevitably focused on the industrial, commercial, and promotional potential of the new Italian fashion, shifted

[53] ASCNMI, b. 57, f. 57-5, Approvazione del verbale della seduta precedente [18 May 1971].

[54] See the documentation related to the legal proceedings started in 1986 by CRAMI against the EFMA (*Ente Fiera Maglieria e Abbigliamento*) in ASCNMI, b. 418, f. 418-1.

the reader's attention in a different direction: it was no longer Florence at the centre of the discussion, but Milan.[55]

Therefore, the capital of Lombardy emerged as the hub of the new Italian fashion, even though comments from the American press and buyers were not always enthusiastic about the collections presented. Noteworthy is the article by Etta Froio from *Women's Wear Daily* dedicated to the first day of the Milan event for the autumn–winter 1975–1976 season, eloquently titled "Milan: sparks but no fireworks".[56] The best received collections were those from Sanlorenzo, Callaghan, and Trell, signed by Walter Albini. However, none of these collections pleased everyone entirely. For instance, the representatives of the American department store I. Magnin were so enthusiastic about Callaghan's garments that they planned to create window displays and advertisements dedicated to the collection and placed exclusive orders for California. On the other hand, the representatives of Neiman Marcus expressed diametrically opposite opinions. Trell's collection, which the sales director of I. Magnin considered the most personality-driven, was deemed "too much layered" by a colleague from Lord & Taylor, who was more impressed by Sanlorenzo's proposal. Callaghan and Albini represented, at that moment, the most avant-garde brand and fashion designer in the pursuit of a new relationship between creativity and industry. Apart from the appreciation for the aesthetic qualities of the collections, buyers' interest went further. They were drawn to what Milan and some of its key figures represented for the future of Italian fashion. The most disruptive innovations of that period, therefore, were not to be found in the collections presented (the conflicting judgements expressed by American buyers could also be interpreted as a sign of Italian fashion in transition, not yet fully convincing international markets). Nor were they found in the mechanism of fashion shows as promotional and commercial tools, even though the structure of those in Milan was completely different from those held in Florence and Rome.

The decision of the CNMI to support the presence of its members at the Milan events therefore represented full recognition of Milan, if not as the future of Italian fashion, at least as a real alternative to Rome and Florence. Although belated, this strategy marked a turning point

[55] ASCNMI, b. 318, f. 318-2, *Women's Wear Daily*, 1 October 1976.

[56] ASCNMI, b. 305, f. 305-2, *Women's Wear Daily*, 27 March 1975.

that legitimized a different understanding of Italian fashion. In reality, *Milanovendemoda* introduced many innovations. Firstly, it was a purely commercial trade show, sponsored by an association—*Assomoda*—whose members were exclusively commercial operators. At *Milanovendemoda*, many fashion shows were 'static', meaning they had no runways, models, or even *couturier(e)s*. The true protagonists of the show were the clothes, displayed inside stands set up in prestigious locations throughout the city or at the *Fiera Campionaria* (Milan Sample Fair), which had over half a century of experience as an exhibition centre for major innovations in many sectors of Italian industry.[57]

Overall, these were unmistakably Milanese venues, deeply rooted in the city's history. The locations were evocative of its past but, at the same time, capable of nurturing its future through pioneering initiatives in the fields of fashion and design. A significant example of this was seen in the 1978 edition, which also included the historic and prestigious Hotel de Milan. Inside the hotel, the installations for the fashion shows were designed by three emerging stars of Italian design: the very young architects Claudio Nardi and Carlo and Claudio Castiglioni, all recent graduates from the Polytechnic of Milan under the guidance of a prominent figure in Italian Brutalism, Vittoriano Viganò. The installations were created using scaffolding poles and joints commonly found on any construction site. They were complemented by sheets that artificially lowered the ceiling height and nets that gathered the clothes. The choice of a highly technical and spartan arrangement intentionally created a contrast between the distinctive features of the new Italian design and the refined style of the Milanese hotel. The simplicity and functionality that characterized the event made the displayed clothes the true protagonists of the space and, therefore, the entire exhibition scene.

During the 1970s, *Milanovendemoda* established itself as the primary showcase for the new Italian fashion. Walter Albini was one of its main protagonists. In 1977, for example, he amazed the audience with an entirely innovative presentation. The chosen setting was an exhibition space in the very central Via Manzoni opened by Giovanni Anselmino, a young collector of contemporary art who, in the preceding years, had hosted exhibitions of significant American artists such as Man Ray, Andy

[57] Longoni (1987) and Masia (2020).

Warhol, and Allan Kaprow.[58] Albini did not present his own collection but instead showcased a series of clothing items borrowed from other fashion designers including Giorgio Armani, Basile, Fiorucci, Krizia, Missoni, Caumont, and Miyake. Those expecting fashion shows with models were disappointed. The setup consisted of panels covered in shiny white plastic material onto which masks moulded from Albini's own face were affixed. The garments were mounted on these panels and were paired with other clothing items and accessories created or collected by Albini from around the world. The objective was not just to present a product but to demonstrate the highly personal way in which he interpreted the works of other fashion designers. The underlying message was clear: "to fully live one's freedom of choice, even in the realm of fashion".[59] This was a new and disruptive approach. Each fashion show presented itself as a distinct proposal of image and style, different from that of other fashion houses and dedicated to a previously identified and selected audience.

These few examples shed light on the main aspects that set *Milanovendemoda* apart from the events in Florence and Rome, which just a few years earlier had celebrated the birth of Italian fashion and its role as a tool for preserving the political, social, and moral status quo. It is easy to understand that the CNMI's opening towards Milan represented a break from the institutional role it had played up to that point and, as we have seen, aimed to find a delicate yet precarious balance. The Milanese fashion shows, therefore, marked a departure from the past, presenting a new Italian fashion that was very different from that of the 1950s. This fashion was more commercial yet closer to the new expressions of art and design, sharing the principle of industrial-scale reproducibility of creative works. It is no coincidence that the fashion designer Giorgio Armani founded his company (together with manager and entrepreneur Sergio Galeotti) in 1975. This is a symbolic date, confirming the central role assumed by Milan, and, as we will see in the following pages, a moment which can be considered the birth of a new Italian fashion system. Armani and many other fashion designers of that generation did not become members of the CNMI. Those who joined soon left. Their disinterest in what was supposed to be the representative body for all of Italian fashion—and

[58] Bortolotti (2019).

[59] ASCNMI, b. 317, f. 317-6, *Informazioni rapide per la stampa*, 18 October 1976.

at that time, the most representative—was therefore another sign of the decline of a top-down governance model that had previously accompanied (and supported) the sector's development but now seemed outdated.

From an institutional perspective, the mid-1970s marked, if not a moment of void, at least a period of metamorphosis and the beginning of a new phase, from which the CNMI itself emerged profoundly changed. There are essentially three events that mark the timing and define the boundaries of this change. First, the decision to encourage members to showcase their collections on the Milanese runways; then, the opening of an office in Milan (where the CNMI would permanently relocate at the end of the 1980s); finally, the election in 1985 of Loris Abate, the first President to come from the business world rather than the political circles in Rome.

In the new context that had emerged, the management of fashion shows became increasingly complex (primarily due to the increasing number of fashion houses participating and the international press accredited to attend the shows) while increasingly focused on purely administrative matters. By the late 1970s, in the city of Milan alone, the schedule of trade events was structured into three distinct yet complementary events. *Milanovendemoda*, a purely commercial event designed for differentiated and qualified apparel by merchandise sector (ready-to-wear, boutiques, knitwear, leather, sportswear, and accessories), had been joined by *Milano Prêt-à-porter* (later *Milano Collezioni*) and *Modit* (Moda Italiana). The first was a promotional event promoted by the CNMI and dedicated to the most prestigious fashion labels, while the second had been initiated in 1978 by the AIIA and the Industrial Association of Knitwear. *Modit* had effectively replaced the SAMIA event in Turin (which was permanently discontinued in 1977) and, in terms of merchandise and schedule, was positioned between *Milanovendemoda* and *Milano Collezioni*. With its multiple events, by the late 1970s, the city of Milan was capable of satisfying a large segment of the demand for ready-made fashion.[60] All these innovations were consolidated in the 1980s, during which Milanese fashion events took off. For instance, in 1984, the autumn edition of *Modit* attracted 255 exhibitors and over 23,000 visitors (a 27% increase on the previous year), including 4,750 from foreign countries (up 11%) and 18,290 from Italy (up 32%). *Milanovendemoda*'s 300 stands, on the

[60] Paris (2006, 480–94).

other hand, attracted 28,350 industry professionals (a 46.4% increase on 1983), including 22,737 Italians (up 50.6%) and 5,613 foreigners (up 31.5%). This trend was confirmed in the following years.[61]

The preparation of the fashion show calendar had become the most important service that the CNMI provided to its members. It was a difficult process, further complicated by the challenging task of finding a compromise between the sometimes irreconcilable needs of fashion houses, the press, and buyers. Other, equally important services were also offered to the industry. For instance, the CNMI carried out a valuable information-sharing activity. On the one hand, it kept its members constantly updated on all major events organized in Italy, thus enabling suitable planning for the production of samples and collections, as well as the promotional phase[62]; on the other hand, it produced periodic reports commenting on the balance of trade for the sector, the result of a cyclical monitoring of market trends.[63] The CNMI was moving away from the regulatory objectives it had pursued previously, gradually transforming itself into something much closer to a business interest association.

Some data may be useful to better understand the impact that the 1970s and 1980s had on the Italian fashion industry. The period of institutional renewal, in fact, coincided with the years of the sector's success in international markets. Exports of textile and clothing industry products grew at an increasing rate and exceeded imports.

Table 3.1 provides a detailed overview of foreign trade for the period 1970–2000 and suggests interesting considerations. The first concerns the comparison between total balances (column G) and the trade balances with foreign countries for textile and clothing industry products (column H). The former were negative until the early 1990s, while the latter have always been positive and steadily increasing. The second reflection relates to the exports of textile and clothing industry products, which increased in absolute value (column E) but showed a generally decreasing trend in relation to total exports (column F), the result of significant growth in the latter (column D). It is worth noting that the peak reached

[61] Zincone (1985).

[62] E.g. see ASCNMI, b. 269, f. 269-4, *Manifestazioni 1972*; b. 272, f. 272-6, *Manifestazioni 1973*; b. 399, f. 399-4, *Manifestazioni 1984*; b. 406, f. 406-1, *Manifestazioni 1985*.

[63] E.g. see ASCNMI, b. 342, f. 342-1; b. 365, f. 365-5, *Bilancia commerciale italiana nel settore tessile, abbigliamento e accessori nel primo semestre del 1979*.

in the early 1970s (12.69%) was nearly matched in the second half of the following decade (12.33%), partially following the events described in the preceding pages. With the exception of the period 1990–1995, textile and clothing industry product exports tripled in the five-year period 1975–1980 and more than doubled in the subsequent 1980–1985 period, taking advantage of the significant growth potential from a low starting point. They then settled into lower but still substantial growth rates, before finally slowing down in the last five years. Additionally, the domestic market performed well. Despite increasing international competition, the percentage of imports of textile and clothing industry products compared to total imports remained stable at between 3.36% and 5.26% (column C).

In the light of these figures, it appears that the dynamics of international trade in Italian fashion were largely indifferent to the institutional crisis that reached its peak between the late 1970s and early 1980s. The analysis of the trade balance thus raises several questions. Did the crisis of the previously existing institutional model release energies trapped in an outdated structure? Had the old model been replaced by new governance models? Can the success of Italian fashion be more generally considered as an outcome of the process of globalization that engulfed markets in

Table 3.1 Italian exports and imports of textile and clothing products, 1970–2000 (millions of eurolira)

Year	*Total imports* A	*Imports of textile products and clothing* B	% C	*Total exports* D	*Exports of textile products and clothing* E	% F	*Total balance* G	*Balance of textile products and clothing* H
1970	4,832	195	4.04%	4,263	541	12.69%	−569	346
1975	13,015	424	3.26%	11,809	1,221	10.34%	−1,206	797
1980	44,190	1,731	3.92%	34,458	3,731	10.83%	−9,732	2,000
1985	89,249	3,750	4.20%	77,326	9,535	12.33%	−11,923	5,785
1990	112,434	5,484	4.88%	105,107	12,827	12.20%	−7,327	7,343
1995	173,354	9,121	5.26%	196,860	22,280	11.32%	23,506	13,159
2000	258,507	12,770	4.94%	260,413	26,733	10.27%	1,906	13,963

Sources Istat, Coeweb—Foreign Trade Statistics; Istat (2006)

the final decades of the last century,[64] rendering institutional efforts to promote and develop the sector unnecessary? To attempt to provide an answer, there are three new elements that emerged forcefully during those years which must be placed at the centre of any analysis: the city of Milan, the new fashion designers (stylists), and the relationship between creativity and industry.

The city of Milan had been leading Italian industrial development since the end of the nineteenth century. In the middle of the following century, Milan was the main contributor to the strong growth experienced by the Italian clothing industry.[65] Between 1951 and 1961, the number of workers in the sector grew from 32,000 to 48,000 individuals (13.7% of the national total of workers). 26,000 of these workers were in Milan. As for ready-made clothes, Milan produced approximately 15% of the country's menswear, 17% of children's, and 24% of women's garments.[66] It is important to stress that such a quantitative development is the result of dynamics that are very different depending on the productive branches. The knitwear industry (underwear and socks) provided the largest contribution to the overall growth of the clothing industry. In the post-war years, the sector's production experienced a strong increase as a result of new dynamics in international markets. During the first half of the 1960s, foreign demand was particularly significant: the value of exports grew more than threefold from 109,035,271 USD in 1960 to almost 352,281,825 USD in 1966. The contribution that Milanese firms made to national production, that in 1966 was 30,000 tonnes of knitwear and 138 million pairs of socks, was 25% and 30%, respectively. These firms were mainly small enterprises which joined a few older and larger companies. As far as commercial activities are concerned, in 1961 in Milan there were 23,911 shops with 68,325 employees; 7,017 of these shops (23,303 employees) sold textiles and ready-to-wear clothes.[67] Until the beginning of the 1950s, ready-made clothes were still produced on an artisan scale using artisan methods, but from the middle of that decade the wide availability of low-cost female labour and the low capital required to start

[64] Crafts and Magnani (2013).

[65] For a more detailed analysis and comparison to Rome and Florence see Merlo and Polese (2006).

[66] Dalmasso (1971, 284–85).

[67] Unione Commercianti della Provincia di Milano (1966).

a firm producing ready-made clothes fuelled the start of a process of industrialization.

In addition to providing an important contribution to the growth of Italian textile and clothing production, Milan played an important role in strengthening the ties between Italian industry and the American market, as shown by the figures concerning trade and especially exports to the United States. The part played by Milan in the growth of the flow of Italian products to the United States is quite clear and well documented, especially for the 1960s.[68] In 1964, Milan's exports reached a value of 1,603 million USD and 2,722 million USD in 1968 (respectively 30.92% and 31.28% of total national exports). The exports of textile, clothing, and leather products accounted for just under 387 million USD (32.8% of total national exports). One-third of Milan's textile exports was made up of synthetic and artificial fibres, a sector in which Milan accounted for 84% of total national commerce. Knitwear ranked second, with 40 million USD (16.6% of total national exports), followed by woollen products with 29 million USD (15% of total Italian exports). Regarding the final destination, exports to the United States represented 23.15% of Italian trade with that country, while 24% of Milanese exports towards the United States was made up of textiles and clothing (second only to the export of machinery). In the same period, Milan was also contributing to the growth of the Italian fashion business in different ways. For example, the city was home to the most important fashion magazines published in Italy.[69] Its pivotal role for the development of Italian fashion was also strengthened by the *Fiera Campionaria* which in 1951 featured the first stand devoted to fashion. In addition to the major Milanese high fashion ateliers, all parts of the fashion business were represented—men's tailors, fur, jewel, leather, and accessory shops—together with numerous textile companies. The specific characteristics of the exhibition stressed the role that Milan was starting to play as the link between the textile industry and the tailoring business, which distinguished it from the other Italian fashion cities.

During the 1950s, Krizia and Missoni began their activities in Milan. They joined renowned fashion houses that produced and marketed high fashion and boutique fashion, such as Enzo, Wanda Roveda, and the

[68] Dalmasso (1971, 342–45).

[69] Carrarini (2003).

previously mentioned Jole Veneziani and Mila Schön. In the 1960s, Cadette, Caumont, Basile, and the aforementioned Callaghan arrived on the scene. Towards the end of the decade, names like Luciano Soprani, Gianni Versace, and Gianfranco Ferré began to make their mark. The documentation submitted to the CNMI as part of their membership applications confirms that these 'names' not only represented the fashion designer but also the fashion house (the company providing stylistic consulting services and/or producing collections) and the associated brand. Archival documentation thus provides further evidence of the fusion of creativity, production, and entrepreneurship upon which Milan built its future as the capital of fashion. It also highlights the establishment of a network of economic and institutional relationships, with the CNMI still coordinating fashion shows and selecting participants.[70]

According to art historian Maria Teresa Olivari Binaghi, 1962 seems to be the year in which the beginnings of all future innovations were concentrated in Milan.[71] Several events marked the beginning of a decade that established Milan at the centre of the new Italian ready-to-wear (prêt-à-porter) scene. For instance, Eva Sabbatini had disrupted traditional Milanese elegance by dressing some members of the upper classes in informal attire, notably the recognizable favourite of the youth, the duffle-coat, during the opening of the La Scala theatre season in Milan. Elio Fiorucci initiated a colour and style revolution by designing brightly coloured plastic boots.[72] Furthermore, an unusual fashion show took place at the Museum of Science, featuring some names that would later achieve great success, including the previously mentioned Enzo, Wanda Roveda, and Krizia. Officially, the production of prêt-à-porter 'made in Milan' made its official debut on April 27, 1971. The occasion was a fashion show held at the *Circolo del Giardino*. During this event, five companies, coordinated by Walter Albini, which had moved away from the Florence runways (Misterfox, Basile, Escargots, Callaghan, and Diamont's), jointly presented their collections. These collections were characterized not only by their aversion to ostentation but also by the high quality of materials and production techniques.

[70] The archival documents refer to ASCNMI, b. 12, f. 12-2; b. 16, f. 16-3 e f. 16-13; b. 14, f. 14-1; b. 22, f. 22-19; b. 23, f. 23-6; b. 26, f. 26-1; b. 27, f. 27-18; b. 29, f. 29-16.

[71] Olivari Binaghi (1996, 531).

[72] Fiorucci (1993) and Owen and Coppola (2017).

The timing of these events indicates a shift in the production landscape surrounding Milanese fashion which was already underway before the crisis that engulfed the Italian clothing industry during the 1970s. The causes of this crisis and its effects, particularly on the large industrial enterprises that had formed and vertically integrated in the 1950s and 1960s, have been discussed in the previous chapters. An analysis of employment dynamics and the number of local units in the industry as a whole and in the textile and clothing sector, succinctly outlined in Tables 3.2 and 3.3, provides further insights to better understand the relationship between the crisis of the 1970s and the industrial and institutional changes in Italian fashion that materialized over the following two decades.

Regarding the workforce, the numbers show that the percentage of those employed in the textile and clothing industries compared to the total employed in manufacturing halved during the second half of the twentieth century. However, these two industries contributed differently to this downsizing. Employment in the textile industry decreased steadily throughout the second half of the last century. The employment trend in the clothing industry aligned with that of Italian industry in general (the positive trend reversed for both, starting in the 1980s). Essentially, for the Italian textile industry, the effects of the crisis of the 1970s were

Table 3.2 Number of workers in the Italian textile and clothing industries, 1951–2001

Economic group	*1951*	*1961*	*1971*	*1981*	*1991*	*2001*
Clothing industry	411,546[a]	513,395	588,499	676,118	644,353	473,785
Textile industry	650,867	598,569	541,030	493,590	384,829	283,087
Total textile and clothing industries	1,062,413	1,111,964	1,129,529	1,169,708	1,029,182	756,862
Total manufacturing industries	3,498,220	4,498,004	5,308,587	6,143,378	5,784,612	5,252,942
%	30	25	21	19	18	14

[a]Including the footwear industry
Sources ISTAT general surveys of industry and services

Table 3.3 Textile and clothing industry local units, 1951–2001

Economic group	*1951*	*1961*	*1971*	*1981*	*1991*	*2001*
Clothing industry	218,602[a]	118,702	97,041	83,282	70,890	53,243
Textile industry	38,683	44,456	49,280	60,061	46,161	26,351
Total textile and clothing industries	257,285	163,158	146,321	143,343	117,051	79,594
Total manufacturing Industries	631,875	609,760	629,759	784,777	862,612	749,815
%	40	26	23	18	13	10

[a]Including the footwear industry
Sources ISTAT general surveys of industry and services

part of a long-term trend characterized by the adoption of labour-saving technologies and the increasing importance of the synthetic and artificial fibre-producing industry, which exacerbated its impact.

With regard to the number of local units, the figures reveal an even more pronounced decline compared to the total number for manufacturing industries. Also in this case, the two industries contributed differently. The textile sector grew until the 1980s, after which it witnessed two decades of decline, partly due to the expulsion of technologically less efficient firms from the market. Conversely, for the clothing industry, the number of local units started decreasing as early as the 1960s, following a trend that the textile and manufacturing industries as a whole also followed in the 1980s and 1990s. For the clothing industry, the crisis of the 1970s was part of a trend of reducing the number of local units that had already begun. In this case too, the units that disappeared from the market were those with the lowest performance. This low efficiency was not limited to technological aspects but mainly included organizational and financial aspects. To a large extent, these were the micro-individual enterprises much more common in the production of clothing than textiles.

A more detailed analysis of the structure of the clothing sector reveals a polarization with a few large enterprises on the one side and many small and medium-sized enterprises on the other.[73] Among these smaller businesses were the workshops which, in the late 1960s and early 1970s,

[73] Paris (2006, 495).

faced a highly unpredictable market which was not yet of international proportions. These firms were more flexible and open to change. The large industrial enterprises, which had already encountered difficulties for a variety of reasons mentioned in previous chapters, returned to prominence later, after the phase of experimentation between creativity and industry had passed. Walter Albini and Giorgio Armani can be considered the archetypes of the first and second phases in the evolution of the relationship between fashion and industry. The outcome of these two complementary phases led to the emergence of *stylism* and the so-called *stylist*. Briefly revisiting the experiences of these two fashion giants allows us to highlight the attributes of this new figure, distinct from the fashion designers who had propelled Italian fashion to success in the preceding decades. At the same time, the trajectory of Albini and Armani can help us understand the role that the stylist might have played, also from an institutional perspective, in both the success of the post-1970s fashion sector and the definitive consolidation of a genuine Italian fashion system.

From the limited available information, it appears that Walter Albini (1941–1983) moved to Paris in 1961 after collaborating with several fashion magazines as an illustrator.[74] The French experience was decisive. Those years marked his apprenticeship and passion for Coco Chanel, considered the one true model of style and elegance. During that period, Albini also created his first complete collection, commissioned by the tailor Gianni Baldini and presented at SAMIA in Turin in 1963. In 1964, he began his collaboration with Krizia, who brought him to Milan where he started designing for other fashion houses such as Billy Ballo, Trell, Cole of California, and Cadette. Another crucial step occurred in 1968, when Albini was introduced to the Callaghan knitwear company, which aimed to expand its market and was looking for a designer to create a complete collection. Albini's contribution was decisive. On the one hand, he prompted Callaghan to modify its machinery according to their projects, and on the other hand, he carried out research on fabrics and colours together with the company's technicians. Also in 1968, he designed five different collections shown in Florence for five different companies: Trell, Krizia, Princess Luciana, Billy Ballo, and Montedoro.

[74] Alfonsi (1974, 19–21), Tutino Vercelloni and Lucchini (1975, 104–19), Mulassano and Castaldi (1979, 45–51), Bianchino (1988), Sozzani and Masunicci (1990), Giordani Aragno, (1997, 12–23, 31–33), Morini (2000, 326–34), Frisa and Tonchi (2010), ASCNMI, b. 39, f. 39–10, *Walter Albini – Clarabella spa, 1978–1983.*

These experiences showed an initial element of novelty. An advocate of a 'total look', Albini also designed fabrics, accessories, glass, furniture, and a variety of other goods.

However, these were the years when the production of collections was linked to the brand of the company or the name of the boutique that commissioned them. The fashion creator remained a mere consultant. Albini realized that to establish his own name, he needed to build a different relationship with the manufacturer. This relationship had to be more equal, which is why Albini decided to become a partner in a small company that produced clothing. This firm was Misterfox, owned by Luciano Papini, with whom Albini worked until 1974, achieving significant recognition. The early 1970s were the years in which Albini created his first highly successful collections: the autumn–winter 1970–1971 collections designed for Montedoro and Misterfox, presented in Florence in 1970. These collections were truly groundbreaking, and their success was repeated in the following years, to the extent that it strained the limited production capacity of some of the companies involved (as in the case of the Anagrafe collection for Misterfox).

By the end of the 1960s, the brief period of experimentation in the collaboration with industry had ended for Albini. These had been years which heralded a series of innovations, not only in style. These new ideas, in addition to subsequent innovations, would prove crucial for the success of Italian fashion as a whole. Eager to make a clean break with the past and to try a new path that would allow him not to spread his ideas across various collections, Albini decided to enter the market with a single strong and recognizable idea which could apply to different products. Applying this new approach, which had already been tested by him in 1968 and called *linea unitaria* for this occasion, in 1971 he designed clothing for five separate fashion houses, each of which specialized in a different product. The collections were designed for Misterfox (women's ready-to-wear), Basile (men's ready-to-wear), Sportfox (shirtmaking), Callaghan (jersey suits), and Escargots (knitwear), but within a unitary project and following a single 'style'. The real innovation, therefore, lay in the approach to creating collections. Albini also decided to abandon the Florentine catwalks, choosing the more dynamic and modern Milan as the venue for his fashion shows. It was another sign of the changes that were also taking place in the geography of Italian fashion. In 1971, along with Papini, Albini also found a solution for the distribution of the new collections: entrusting it to the FTM group, which had introduced the innovative sales formula that concentrated the most innovative Italian and French ready-to-wear brands in a prestigious showroom on Milan's Via della Spiga.

Albini's new approach achieved great success and was maintained for subsequent collections. However, in 1972, the first cracks appeared. The FTM group found many items from that year's collections unsellable and withdrew them from the market without informing Albini, who terminated the contract with the Milanese distributor. Shortly after, Albini also severed ties with Callaghan, Basile, and Escargots—but he did not give up his partnership with Luciano Papini. This choice, however, foreshadowed other innovations. Up until that point, the label of each clothing item always featured the wording "Walter A. for", followed by the name of the company for which the stylist had designed the collection. After the experience with the *linea unitaria*, in 1972 Albini created his own line and a personal brand designed to clearly and unequivocally distinguish his creations. With the help of Sidney and Joan Berstein, owners of the London boutique Browns, the new WA logo was first used in December of that year, in a small fashion show featuring clothing produced exclusively for Misterfox.

The first true collection bearing the WA brand was launched in 1973, the year when Albini opened his own showroom in Milan. The chosen location was the renowned Caffè Florian, located in Piazza San Marco in Venice, which was followed by a similar presentation in New York. Albini's WA collection definitively consolidated his image as a stylist and opened doors to international markets. Simultaneously, in the Milan showroom, Albini showcased another collection, once again for Misterfox, introducing another innovation in the relationship between creation and industry: the formula of a first line with a strong and driving image, bearing the stylist's brand and designed for a select clientele, financially supported by a second collection intended for the general public, to be marketed under the company's brand. However, without the support of a solid production and commercial structure, in 1974 Albini was unable to prepare the collections in time for the presentations, instead organizing an exhibition of his designs in Milan. The die was cast, though, and Albini's approach would later be followed by many others.

Also in 1974, the collaboration with Luciano Papini experienced a crisis. Their company was liquidated, forcing Albini to leave the Milan showroom. Plagued by financial problems, after some trips to the East, Albini returned to Milan and decided to take on high fashion directly, seeking to impose his own language and a new production scheme, which did not involve the establishment of an atelier but rather the production of prototypes and models to be sold to dressmakers, stores, and boutiques who would then make them to measure. This new concept materialized in the presentation of two collections on the runways in Rome, but it had no future. After other brief and unsuccessful collaborations with the industry, in the early 1980s Albini permanently retreated into stylistic consultancy.

Albini was a man of exceptional stylistic talents and extraordinary commercial and entrepreneurial insights which he developed during a period of crisis and restructuring of the clothing industry. These were precursors of some of the most important strategic solutions adopted by fashion companies in the 1980s. For this reason, Albini is considered the progenitor of a generation of stylists who, in the last two decades of the twentieth century, transformed clothing into a product of industrial design, propelling Italian ready-to-wear to the top of the international market. Other important Italian stylists followed suit, thus confirming, by the start of the 1970s, the role of the stylist as the unifier of the Italian fashion system.[75] *Stilismo* emerged as the ideal tool for achieving definitive leadership in taste-making while significantly reducing fashion risk. The only possible way an individual company could manage well-developed and complex demand rationally was to create its own specific market segment. Young consumers had opened a new market with very specific requirements. Delivering styles that proposed to better satisfy the tastes of the young, the stylist gradually came to dominate this large slice of the market. Their strategy was to identify a particular brand with a clear and easily distinguishable style, thus making it much easier to insert new stylistic elements into a collection while controlling the risks associated with the volatility of fashion. In essence, style linked a stable brand with unstable fashion and the stylist became the point of connection between these elements and the requirements of both industrial production and consumers. The rise of the stylist signalled a new way of thinking about fashion that was different from both French prêt-à-porter and Italian *alta moda pronta*: fashion was no longer imposed on the consumer; rather, the consumer was presented with a series of options from which to choose, options that themselves were more than just clothing for they represented lifestyles.

[75] ASCNMI, bb. 185–87, 199–202.

The relevance of the stylist to the Italian fashion system is enormous. Linking lifestyles with personal cultural choices, the identities of the stylist and his creations merged. Mythologized by the press, which presented biographies of stylists as comparable to those of true artists, they became cultural reference points. As their reputation surpassed that of the industry for which they worked, fashion became a genuine cultural product. The identification of a particular style with the designer label opened up possibilities for a personalized 'total look', which could encompass a host of new consumer goods outside of the textile–clothing sphere. Indeed, opportunities were potentially endless, ranging from cosmetics and jewellery to household goods, pet accessories, and even the designer label holidays that have become popular in recent years. Expert in the technical–organizational aspects of the industry and in the requirements of the public, coordinator of the entire production chain from the selection of raw materials to the definition of marketing strategies for finished products, creator of styles and lifestyles, the stylist managed a plurality of functions and thus could drive the integration of processes as well as diversification of products. In this way, the figure of the stylist both represented the cohesive force of the whole fashion system and became the guarantor of an unprecedented unity of functions.[76]

In the mid-1970s, Amos Ciabattoni acknowledged the existence of the new professional category of the 'stylist', clearly distinct from *couturier(e)s*, tailors, and generic fashion creators.[77] Ciabattoni's definition emphasized the social function of the stylist, capable of understanding and interpreting the dissatisfaction of consumers disillusioned with high fashion and disoriented by the excesses of the phenomenon known as *antimoda* (anti-fashion).[78] Recent studies view the social function of the stylist as inseparable from that of the clothing designer.[79] Stylists have been also deemed as the modern version of medieval *clerici vagantes* as they do not form lasting bonds with one or more industrial companies, considering the industrial partner an essential component for the continuous renewal of collections.[80] To these peculiarities, another

[76] Paris, (2010, 550–51).

[77] Ciabattoni (1976, 185).

[78] Gnecchi Ruscone (1987).

[79] Volontè (2008).

[80] Olivari Binaghi (1996, 537).

must be added, which was still premature in the mid-1970s. Sociological analyses and the interpretative categories of costume history and the history art both failed to capture this particular aspect which has also been overlooked by economic and business historians. Stylists were, in fact, creators and negotiators of new rules, thus playing an 'institutional' role that contributed to the definitive consolidation of the Italian fashion system, with the stylist as the guarantor of the system's stability. This function was never fully developed by Albini, perhaps due to his premature death, but it becomes evident when analysing the stages that led Giorgio Armani and his fashion company to establish themselves among the major international players in the industry.

Giorgio Armani is representative of the new generation of stylists who laid the foundations for the most renowned Italian fashion companies.[81] Giorgio Armani Spa was founded in 1975, when Walter Albini's career was declining. Armani had entered the world of fashion many years earlier, in 1957, after leaving medical school to take up a position as a buyer for the department store La Rinascente. His initial experience was not positive. According to an interview he gave to the American magazine Time in 1982, he helped create ambitious window displays featuring products from foreign and exotic locations such as Latin America, India, and Japan. However, this endeavour was a failure, to the extent that Armani was transferred to the Fashion and Style department, where "employees who had nothing to do were sent". After spending seven years there, in 1964, a La Rinascente manager arranged an interview for him with Nino Cerruti. Cerruti, owner of one of the largest Italian firms producing men's clothing, was looking for an assistant for a new fashion line. To provide Armani with some on-the-job training, Cerruti sent him to spend a month in a factory where, as Armani recalled in the interview, he "fell in love with textiles and began to understand the work behind each yard of fabric".[82]

In 1975, Armani, who in the meantime had left Cerruti, presented his first spring–summer collection of men's and women's ready-to-wear in Milan. At that time, he also worked as a freelance designer for GFT. As one of the largest Italian clothing firms with the most modern organizational and technical structure, GFT provided Armani with manufacturing skills that allowed him to fully unleash his creative talent. The connection

[81] White (2000), Mohlo (2006), Celant (2007), and Potvin (2012).

[82] Cocks et al. (1982).

with GFT was important not only for the career of the Milanese fashion designer but also for the entire Italian fashion system.

The partnership between Armani and GFT began in 1978. The first result was the industrial version of the unstructured jacket, which Albini had previously devised but failed to turn into a product innovation. Armani, however, continued to increase the quality of industrially produced clothing. Usually made with traditional menswear fabrics, the women's unstructured jacket—like the men's version designed by Armani just a few years before—looked intentionally imperfect and creased, an effect obtained thanks to a mix of provocative tactics such as buttons moved down, lapels with a lower notch, sloped shoulders, lining and padding removed, and a masterly combination of nuanced tones and soft fabrics. The stylistic details which distinguished the unstructured jacket had precisely the function of making faults and weaknesses which were peculiar to industrial manufacturing fashionable. Buttons moved down and lapels with a lower notch made the inaccuracy of finishing touches less evident, while shoulders sloped and lining and padding were missing—both traditionally considered to be evidence of imperfect cutting and rough sizing—giving the outfit a particular allure. Thanks to nuanced tones, unevenly dyed fabrics became a distinctive feature of Armani's style. In reality, the fashion designers' creativity glamorized unfashionable standardized clothing.[83]

Another aspect to consider is the type of partnership that bound Armani to GFT. In 1978, Armani signed a licensing agreement with GFT, which included both the Giorgio Armani *white label* diffusion line (a secondary line intended to reach customers with lower price points) and the more exclusive Giorgio Armani *black label* collection. In 1979, Armani and GFT created a joint venture in the United States (the Giorgio Armani Men's Wear Corporation). The new corporation would serve to introduce Armani's labels to a broader North American audience and would be responsible for the manufacture and distribution of the new label *Giorgio Armani Le Collezioni*. In 1983, a further contract was signed to produce *Mani*, a second diffusion line of menswear for Canada and the United States and of womenswear for the European market.[84]

[83] Merlo (2011, 359).

[84] Merlo and Perugini (2020, 56–57).

The comparison between Albini and Armani allows us to better understand the reasons why both the planning efforts made by fashion institutions in the 1960s and the attempts pursued in the same years to develop a luxury ready-to-wear production failed. As highlighted in the previous section, the crux of the matter was flexibility, typical of a creative industry especially in the emerging phase of its lifecycle. Both planning and luxury ready-to-wear production lacked the flexibility that was essential to meet the notably polymorphous fashion trends of the time (and the so-called fashion risk that ensued). However, if flexibility was better suited to small and medium-sized enterprises compared to larger ones, only the latter possessed the necessary industrial capabilities, in terms of technical and technological assets, organizational structures, and financial resources, in order to introduce elements of flexibility into large-scale industrial production. The figure of the stylist emerged from this contradiction, i.e., from experimenting with collaborative relationships with small enterprises characterized by a strong propensity for innovation on the one hand, and with large industrial enterprises on the other. This revealed the limitations of the former as stable industrial partners capable of managing the whims and excesses of creative genius within enduring collaborative relationships, not limited to ad hoc consultations and commissions, and the potential of the latter, capable of transforming stylistic innovations into product innovations and giving the stylist the necessary know-how to transition from a mere consultant to an entrepreneur and manager of creativity.

The contracts entered into between GFT and Armani, as well as those with other renowned stylists such as Ungaro and Valentino, marked the beginning of a new phase in the history of the relationship between creativity and industry. These were licensing contracts that included specific rules and penalties for non-compliance and violations, and they can also be considered the instrument used to consolidate the Italian fashion system. The clothing was marketed exclusively using the stylist's brand and not that of the manufacturing company. The production process was under the exclusive control of the stylist, who could have halted it at any time if the product was deemed not in line with his/her own standards. The costs of promoting the collections were entirely borne by the company, but the budget was independently managed by the stylist, who received royalties equal to a fixed percentage of the entire budget and a variable percentage based on net sales. The stylist also benefited from a clause that protected him/her from fluctuations in sales, pre-approved all advertising and promotional campaigns, and enjoyed full commercial autonomy. In essence, the stylist managed his/her own boutiques independently of the agreement with the industrial partner. As in the case of Armani and GFT, they were not obliged to sell the collections produced by GFT in their own boutiques, but could sell their own collections produced by other companies. Regarding the distribution channels regulated by the agreement, such as American department stores which represented the main sales channel for Armani collections produced by GFT, the stylist could use them to promote and market his own high fashion collections as well. No percentage of sales was paid to the industrial partner for these collections. Having been refined in the realm of clothing, these licensing agreements were subsequently extended to a wide range of other products, from accessories to cosmetics and furniture.

For the stylists, such licensing agreements were a goldmine and an extraordinary entrepreneurial and managerial learning opportunity. For clothing manufacturing companies, however, they involved enormous risks which were justified by the forecasts of expansion in the American market, which exceeded those of the sluggish European context. Thanks in part to favourable exchange rate dynamics, sales exceeded even the most optimistic expectations. Licensing agreements managed to lift industrial companies out of the quagmire of the 1970s crisis and ushered in a new phase not only for the clothing industry but for the entire Italian fashion industry. From industrial enterprises that invested in stylists as a new type of human capital, there was a transition to true fashion companies that transformed industrial enterprise into an exclusive production asset, often prompting the stylist to acquire it.

The overturning of the status quo described in these pages provides some insights into possible answers to the questions which were previously raised. Certainly, the globalization of markets had created a favourable environment for the international success of Italian fashion, which only some of the 'old' institutions accommodated by transforming themselves into professional, promotional, and commercial service agencies. The institutional vacuum that was thus created was filled by the stylist, the unexpected winner of the countless disputes that had characterized the relationships between the representative institutions of Italian fashion during the 1950s and 1960s. The stylist had not only played a social function—a function partly shared by the generations of *couturier(e)s* who preceded them. At the same time, they did not limit themselves to being the designer who transformed clothing into a product of industrial design—a characteristic that they shared with designers already active in a wide range of sectors (including clothing). Their prerogative lies more in their institutional function. In other words, stylists established themselves as the linchpin of the renewed Italian fashion system, a new entity capable of setting the rules of the game and around whom, starting in the 1970s, the foundations for the development of the Italian fashion industry and the international success of 'Made in Italy' had been laid, not only in the field of clothing.

References

Alfonsi, Maria Vittoria. 1974. *I grandi personaggi della moda. Incontri con Vittoria Alfonsi*. Bologna: Cappelli.

Amica. 1965. "I guardaroba di Amica." *Amica* 4 (38) (19 September): 49.

Bianchino, Gloria, ed. 1988. *Walter Albini*. Parma: CSAC dell'Università.

Bortolotti, Maria Pia. 2019. *Inventario eredità giacente Luciano Anselmino*. Milan: Archivio di Stato di Milano.

Bruno, Amelia. 1967. "Una lezione di vendita?" *L'Abbigliamento Italiano* 7 (12) (December): 10, 18.

Calandri, Nanda. 1971. "Ottanta milioni d'arancio e beige." *Il Messaggero*, 14 April.

Capalbi, Franca. 1962. "Crisi o momento di disagio?" *L'Abbigliamento Italiano* 4 (4) (May–June): 7–8.

Capalbi, Franca. 1966. "Bella e dannata. L'alta moda e il suo pubblico eletto." *L'Abbigliamento Italiano* 6 (12) (December): 2, 4.

Carrarini, Rita. 2003. "La stampa di moda dall'Unità ad oggi." In *La Moda*, Storia d'Italia, Annali 19, edited by C.M. Belfanti and F. Giusberti, 796–834. Turin: Einaudi.

Cecchi, Marina. 1968. "Tutte le donne hanno il diritto di vestirsi bene, anche quelle che non possono spendere molto." *L'Abbigliamento Italiano*, 10 (1) (January): 21.

Celant, Germano, ed. 2007. *Giorgio Armani*. New York: The Solomon R. Guggenheim Foundation.

Ciabattoni, Amos. 1976. *Il sistema moda*. Turin: Editoriale Valentino.

Cocks, Jay, Georgia Harbison, and Wilton Wynn. 1982. "Giorgio Armani: Suiting Up for Easy Street." *Time*, 5 April.

Coleman, Elizabeth A. 1989. *The Opulent Era: Fashions of Worth, Doucet and Pingat*. New York: The Brooklyn Museum/Thames and Hudson.

Crafts, Nicholas, and Marco Magnani. 2013. "The Golden Age and the Second Globalization in Italy." In *The Oxford Handbook of Italian Economy Since Unification*, edited by G. Toniolo, 69–107. Oxford: Oxford University Press.

Dalmasso, Etienne. 1971. *Milan capitale éeconomique de l'Italie*. Paris: Éditions Ophrys.

De Marly, Diana. 1980. *The History of Haute Couture: 1850–1950*. London: Batsford.

Ente Italiano della Moda. 1976. *La moda nell'economia italiana. Atti della 1. Conferenza nazionale della moda", Torino, 20–21 Maggio 1975*. Turin: Ente Italiano della Moda.

Fiorucci, Elio. 1993. *Challenges of Plastic*. Milan: Half Moon.

Frisa, Maria Luisa, and Tonchi, Stefano. 2010. *Walter Albini and His Times: All Power to the Imagination*. Venice: Marsilio.

Froio, Etta. 1975. "Milan: Sparks But No Fireworks." *Women's Wear Daily*, 27 March.

Giordani Aragno, Bonizza. 1997. *Callaghan, 1966. La nascita del prêt-à-porter italiano*. Milan: Mazzotta.

Gnecchi Ruscone, Alessandra. 1987. "L'antimoda. Esempi milanesi." In *La moda italiana*. Vol. II. *Dall'antimoda allo stilismo*, edited by G. Butazzi and A. Mottola Molfino, 46–63. Milan: Electa.

Grumbach, Didier. 2008. *Histoires de la mode*. Paris: Regard.

Informazioni EIM. 1969. "AIIA. Il IV Congresso di Montecatini." *Informazioni EIM* 11 (November–December): 6–7.

Informazioni EIM. 1970. "Coordinamento." *Informazioni EIM* 15 (July–August): 12–13.

Informazioni EIM. 1971. "Coordinamento tra l'alta moda, l'industria della confezione e l'industria tessile." *Informazioni EIM* 19 (March–April): 5–12.

Istat. 2006. *L'interscambio commerciale italiano: una nuova base informativa per le analisi di lungo periodo. Anni 1970–2005*. Rome: ISTAT.

L'Abbigliamento Italiano. 1963a. "Il couturier Dessès passa alla confezione." *L'Abbigliamento Italiano* (November–December): 9.

L'Abbigliamento Italiano. 1963b. "Nuove prospettive per i figurinisti francesi del prêt-à-porter." *L'Abbigliamento Italiano* (November–December): 29.

L'Abbigliamento Italiano. 1969. "Coordinare i coordinatori." *L'Abbigliamento Italiano* 11 (11) (November): 1–2.

Lipovetsky, Gilles. 1987. *L'empire de l'éphèmere*. Paris: Gallimard.

Longoni, Giuseppe Maria. 1987. *La Fiera nella storia di Milano*. Milan: Motta.

Masia, Luca. 2020. *La Fiera di Milano: 1920–2020 cento anni, infinite storie*. Milan: Skyra.

Massai, Elisa. 1971. "Finalmente d'accordo alta moda e confezione." *Corriere della Sera*, 14 April.

Merlo, Elisabetta. 2003. *Moda italiana. Storia di un'industria dall'Ottocento a oggi*. Venice: Marsilio.

Merlo, Elisabetta. 2011. "Italian Fashion Business: Achievements and Challenges (1970s–2000s)." *Business History* 53 (3): 344–62.

Merlo, Elisabetta, and Polese Francesca. 2006. "Turning Fashion into Business. The Emergence of Milan as International Fashion Hub." *Business History Review* 80 (3): 415–47.
Merlo, Elisabetta, and Mario Perugini. 2020. "Making Italian Fashion Global: Brand Building and Management at Gruppo Finanziario Tessile (1950s–1990s)." *Business History* 62 (1): 42–69.
Messina, Rietta. 1987. "L'abbigliamento femminile italiano: un prodotto industriale di successo." In *La Moda Italiana*, vol. II *Dall'antimoda allo stilismo*, edited by G. Buttazzi and A. Mottola Molfino, Milan: Electa.
Ministero dell'Industria, del Commercio e dell'Artigianato. 1969. *Atti del comitato consultivo della moda*. Turin: Ente Italiano della Moda.
Mohlo, Renata. 2006. *Essere Armani: Una biografia*. Milan: Baldini Castoldi Dalai.
Morini, Enrica. 2000. *Storia della moda XVIII–XX secolo*. Milan: Skira.
Mossetti, Claudio A. 1967. "Dove incomincia la moda?" *L'Abbigliamento Italiano* 7 (1) (January): 9, 12.
Mulassano, Adriana, and Alfa Castaldi. 1979. *I Mass-Moda. Fatti e personaggi dell'Italian look*. Florence: Spinelli.
Olivari Binaghi, Maria Teresa. 1996. "La moda: le tendenze." In *Storia di Milano. Il Novecento*, vol. XVIII, t. 3, 496–563. Rome: Istituto della Enciclopedia Italiana Treccani.
Owen, David, and Coppola, Sofia. 2017. *Fiorucci*. New York: Rizzoli.
Palmer, Alexandra. 2001. *Couture & Commerce: The Transatlantic Fashion Trade in the 1950s*. Vancouver: UBC Press in association with the Royal Ontario Museum.
Paris, Ivan. 2006. *Oggetti cuciti: l'abbigliamento pronto in Italia dal primo dopoguerra agli anni Settanta*. Milan: Franco Angeli.
Paris, Ivan. 2010. "Fashion as a System. Changes in Demand as the Basis for the Establishment of the Italian Fashion System (1960–1970)." *Enterprise & Society* 11 (3): 524–59.
Piccoli, Laura B. 1969a. "Il coordinamento. La parola all'Alta Moda." *L'Abbigliamento Italiano* 11 (6) (June): 5, 10.
Piccoli, Laura B. 1969b. "A che punto siamo con il coordinamento?" *L'Abbigliamento Italiano* 11 (10) (October): 7, 26.
Piccoli, Laura B. 1969c. "Il coordinamento." *L'Abbigliamento Italiano* 11 (11) (November): 5, 17.
Piccoli, Laura B. 1969d. "Coordinamento: verso il traguardo?" *L'Abbigliamento Italiano* 11 (12) (December): 3–4.
Potvin, John. 2012. *Giorgio Armani: Empire of the Senses*. Aldershot: Ashgate.
Pouillard, Véronique. 2016. "Managing Fashion Creativity: The History of the Chambre Syndicale de la Couture Parisienne During the Interwar Period." *Investigaciones de Historia Económica* 12 (2): 76–89.

Ricca, Giuliana. 1968. "I problemi dell'alta moda." *Informazioni EIM* (1) (March–April): 16–17.
Robiola, Elsa. 1967. "Rose e spine nel prêt-à-porter." *L'Abbigliamento Italiano* 7 (3) (March): 5–6.
Robiola, Elsa. 1968. "*Confini* da delimitare per la nostra moda." *L'Abbigliamento Italiano* 10 (11) (November): 1, 16.
Robiola, Elsa. 1969. "Esame di coscienza dell'alta moda." *L'Abbigliamento Italiano* 11 (3) (March): 7–8
Robiola, Elsa. 1970. "*Roma: alta moda italiana primavera-estate 1970*." *L'Abbigliamento Italiano* 12 (2) (February): 6, 28.
Robiola, Elsa. 1971. "Non essere profeti in patria." *L'Abbigliamento Italiano* 13 (9) (September): 3, 6.
Ronco, Giacomo. 1971. "I problemi produttivi connessi con il cambiamento della moda." *Tecnica della Confezione* (March–April): 48–55.
Sozzani, Carla, and Anna Masunicci. 1990. *Walter Albini*. Milan: Carla Sozzani.
Tutino Vercelloni, Isa, and Flavio Lucchini. 1975. *Milano Fashion*. Milan: Condé Nast.
Unione Commercianti della Provincia di Milano. 1966. *Noi commercianti: Bilancio del ventennale 1945–1965*. Milan: S. Print.
Volontè, Paolo. 2008. *Vita da stilista. Il ruolo sociale del fashion designer*. Milan: Mondadori.
White, Nicola. 2000. *Giorgio Armani*. London: Carlton.
Zincone, Bruno. 1971. "Gava: Una funzione-guida per l'industria tessile." *Il Tempo*, 28 May.
Zincone, Rosaria. 1985. "Moda: i primati reggono." *Il Sole 24 Ore*, 9 October.

Conclusions

Defining the Italian fashion system, identifying its peculiarities, and clarifying its historical background are the common thread of this book, which has found a possible interpretive key in the role played by fashion institutions. Our intention is to collect the results of years of research and provide new areas for reflection, fostering the relationship between two disciplinary fields—economic history and fashion history—that have only recently begun to engage in dialogue.

The combination of fashion and institutions is far from intuitive. Yet, fashion itself is a social institution deeply rooted in time and space, and therefore profoundly influenced by the historical context. For this reason, this book first reconstructs the intricate economic, social, and cultural fabric within which what is now referred to as *Italian fashion* emerged. Although its birth is conventionally dated to the early 1950s, it was during the 1970s that the industry established itself as a homogeneous reality, defined by a fully integrated system in terms of structure and market image. From that point onwards, the fashion industry rapidly solidified as one of the (few) clusters in which Italy can still boast a significant international competitive advantage.

To explain this acceleration, the lexicon of fashion included two new terms: *stilismo* (stylism) and *stilista* (stylist). As this book clarifies, the most concise and widely used definition of a *stilista*, namely as a fashion designer, is also the most complex. What are the functions of a fashion designer? For those who emerged starting from the 1970s, fashion design

E. Merlo and I. Paris, *The Italian Fashion System*, Palgrave Studies in Economic History, https://doi.org/10.1007/978-3-031-52375-5

has not been merely about sketches. Designing fashion is, rather, about understanding clothing as a product of industrial design. Consequently, this means creating a unified process that spans from a creative idea to a broader range of industrial products and then to the final market. The creativity of an idea is not measured by its originality alone. What perhaps matters most is the ability to sense and interpret that which the consumer sometimes doesn't even know they desire.

The commercial success of a creative idea also depends on the collaboration between the designer and a company, which involves the designer's capacity to communicate with the industrial partner and the company's ability to interpret the idea to transform it, through materials, colours, shapes, seams, dyeing processes, weaving, manufacturing, and finishing (i.e., through the production process) into a product that represents the 'style' of the fashion designer (also a result of personal cultural choices) and the (changing) tastes of the final consumer. Promotion, marketing, and distribution finally link production to the market. Within this framework, the brand represents the element that uniquely identifies the entire process and ensures its coherence.

The stylist (in collaboration with the company) was therefore central to the consolidation of the Italian fashion system, a necessary precondition for the global success achieved by Italian fashion in the final three decades of the twentieth century. The role of the stylist is multifaceted. All its characteristics have not been adequately highlighted and explored yet. The role of the stylist is not confined to his/her social function as an anticipator, interpreter, and spokesperson of economic and social transformations and his/her impact on consumer choices, nor is it limited to being a designer and guarantor of the unity and cohesion of collections differentiated by target market or a broader range of diversified products. The implicit novelty in the role of the stylist can be fully understood by considering their institutional function, namely as creators of new rules that impact the behaviours and relationships among all actors in the production chain, thus redefining the boundaries and the structure of the fashion system itself.

During the 1970s, the stylist introduced innovations that this book considers fundamental for the formation of the Italian fashion system. In particular, starting from the 1970s, the Italian fashion system developed around the clauses of licensing contracts (which by nature were continuously evolving) rather than the regulations of the statutes of the various fashion organizations active in the previous decades. The latter proved unable to adapt as effectively as the former to the changes in the environment in which they operated. Unlike the French experience, which featured the *Chambre Syndicale de la Haute Couture*, the Italian situation lacked a unified institutional body to represent the interests of the multitude of actors within the sector and regulate and manage areas of utmost importance for learning and passing on of technical knowledge and managerial culture. The *Camera Nazionale della Moda Italiana* (National Chamber of Italian Fashion), the only body to survive the turbulence of the 1960s and 1970s, followed a path that was more similar to a business interest association than a regulatory and governing body for the sector. Consequently, the Italian fashion system, unlike that in France, was effectively a *headless* system, with autonomous and original characteristics, which found in stylists and licensing contracts the actors and instruments needed to consolidate its position in international markets.

The institutional role taken on by the stylist was crucial in setting the Italian *clothing industry* on a new course. In those years, the foundations were laid for its transformation into a true *fashion industry*. The phenomenon of stylism made the Italian fashion system a unique competitive entity during the challenging process of globalization of the late twentieth century. However, it also conferred fragility and vulnerability, obscured by the commercial successes achieved in international markets but undeniable when comparing many Italian fashion companies with the large French luxury conglomerates (of which, incidentally, many of the former are now part). The result is a clear disparity in favour of those large groups, confirmed by dimensional indicators. However, in addition to the presence of a production organization that is currently unmatched elsewhere, the capacity of Italian companies to control niche markets emerged—markets which luxury conglomerates can only enter by acquiring these very companies.

Equating the stylist with an institution is rather hazardous, as the concept of an institution risks being diluted, and that of a stylist distorted. We are fully aware that such a choice may attract criticism. However, the aim of this book is to go beyond the well-established explanations for the rise of Italian fashion to an international standing. Starting from the assumption that institutions and institutional change are central to explaining the peculiarity and development of the Italian fashion system, this book highlights the role of the stylist as a negotiator of new rules and the licensing contract as the means used to implement them.

Index

E. Merlo and I. Paris, *The Italian Fashion System*, Palgrave Studies in Economic History, https://doi.org/10.1007/978-3-031-52375-5

D

E

F

G

H

I

K

GPSR Compliance
The European Union's (EU) General Product Safety Regulation (GPSR) is a set of rules that requires consumer products to be safe and our obligations to ensure this.

If you have any concerns about our products, you can contact us on

ProductSafety@springernature.com

In case Publisher is established outside the EU, the EU authorized representative is:

Springer Nature Customer Service Center GmbH
Europaplatz 3
69115 Heidelberg, Germany

www.ingramcontent.com/pod-product-compliance
Ingram Content Group UK Ltd.
Pitfield, Milton Keynes, MK11 3LW, UK
UKHW020836290926
15470UKWH00004B/1385
* 9 7 8 3 0 3 1 5 2 3 7 4 8 *